FOOTPRINTS

Tales from Times Past

FOOTPRINTS

Tales from Times Past

An Anthology

Edited by

LOUISE MENGELKOCH

PORTLAND • OREGON
INKWATERPRESS.COM

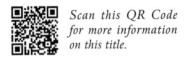

*Scan this QR Code
for more information
on this title.*

Publisher: Inkwater Press | www.inkwaterpress.com

ISBN-13 978-1-62901-572-9 | ISBN-10 1-62901-572-5

1 3 5 7 9 10 8 6 4 2

Dedication

For Ronald Talney, who worked for years as an unpaid volunteer to facilitate the memoir classes that made this book possible and who continues to love hearing our stories

Contents

"We're conditioned to think that our lives revolve around great moments. But great moments often catch us unaware—beautifully wrapped in what others may consider a small one."

Kent Nerburn
*Make Me an Instrument of Your Peace:
Living in the Spirit of the Prayer of St. Francis*

Who We Are: An Introduction

By Louise Mengelkoch

I BELIEVE IT WAS A COLD JANUARY DAY OF 2015 THAT I ATTENDED my first memoir class at the Lake Oswego Adult Community Center. I'd never met Ron Talney, the instructor, nor did I know anybody in the group. I was a transplanted Minnesotan who'd moved far from home to follow a daughter and her family. I felt somehow that my life was marching on too fast for me to reflect on it, and that I needed to start documenting how I got to where I was.

It was a good decision.

Ron had a gentle, quiet way about him that brought out the best in all of us oldsters, who ranged in age from about fifty to more than ninety. The format was deceptively simple: each week, everyone who wanted to do so would read for about five to ten minutes and we would all respond. There was no penalty for not having written, but, amazingly, that seldom happened. We wrote like maniacs because we all wanted to hear what others would say about our stories. Sometimes we wrote such long pieces that we would have to end with a cliff-hanger and continue the next week.

There were no grades, no "corrections." We sometimes brought in show and tell – a book we enjoyed, a photo to accompany our stories, suggestions and news items regarding memoir—but for the most part we just read and talked. Some members of the group, I discovered, were five-year veterans or even longer. Every session, a few would leave and a few new ones would join us, but the format stayed the same.

We realized that, in some ways, we knew more about each other than our closest loved ones. It was part therapy, part creative enterprise, part problem-solving and part fun. Sometimes people would leave after the first class because they expected to "learn" about memoir writing. They didn't know how to start, I guess. But most people caught on pretty fast and were hooked. The demand became so great that Ron had to teach two sections, so I offered to take one of them. We still have a waiting list.

Several of the writers represented in this anthology have commented on how this class is the most important two hours of their week. I would agree. What became clear to me is that these late-blooming writers deserved a wider audience. These stories have a range and authenticity to them that makes them resonate with young and old alike. They challenge stereotypes with their insight about how and why we became who we are. They recount adventures, mishaps and sorrows that we somehow survived. They shine with a sense of humor that makes them disarming.

We hope you like our little book. And I hope, personally, that it inspires you to think about documenting some of the shining moments of your own life for those who come after you, but mostly just for you. You'll be amazed at how it helps you understand the shape and meaning of your life, which may help you live the rest of your time on earth with more depth and pleasure.

Louise Mengelkoch
April 2018

The Moments of Our Lives: Thoughts on the Writing of Memoir

By Ronald Talney

THERE WAS A TIME WHEN THE WRITING OF ONE'S MEMOIRS WAS the work of former presidents and retired generals. A time to retire to the newly constructed presidential library and attempt to reframe an otherwise failed time in office, or capture victory from the jaws of defeat. But times have changed and ordinary folk are now writing about their lives. About their time on this earth. An insight into the years during which they lived. They are writing themselves into the history of their time.

I think we all have a basic need to mark our time on earth in some way. To leave some footprint that others may follow and know we were here. To know something of what pleased us, what hurt us, what wins and losses we endured. What lessons we learned. Something other than just a grave marker to say we were here.

And what of readers? Why has memoir writing become

such a popular genre in the last ten to fifteen years? I am convinced it is because our lives, however ordinary, well told, have the ring of truth to them. That which is said to be true seems to attract readers. While memoir writers may utilize fictional techniques at times, memoir at its best has the ring of truth. Admittedly, some folks live through perilous times and survive. And that fascinates us. Some folks have overcome the odds of cancer or some other frequently terminal illness and made a life for themselves. Or dealt with a childhood of neglect or abuse. Or escaped a stormy and dangerous marriage. Or survived the horrors of war. Overcome an addiction. We have an inherent need to hear their true stories, learn from them and draw courage and inspiration from them.

But what of those of us who, unfortunately for our purposes, have lived happy childhoods and enjoyed long and enduring marriages, and reasonably satisfying careers in our adult lives? We whose time on earth has been blessed in so many ways? Our trials and tribulations seem trivial at best. What do we have to say that would be of interest to a general readership? Or even to our families? More than you might think.

Each of us has an insider's view of history in the making. In school we study history by reading of the monumental events that have changed the course of human existence. The dates of wars, great inventions, natural disasters. But what would we give to have an insider's view of how it was to live, for example, in the Elizabethan age in Jolly Olde England? Or ancient Rome? Or the early days of the forming of the United States? Not the life of a royal, or an emperor, or a drafter of the Constitution, but the life of an ordinary person. To have a day-to-day account of the perils and rewards of a common life? That is what we can provide to our children, grandchildren and future generations. How it was to live before flight was the norm, to have lived through the Great Depression, WWII the Vietnam War era, the civil rights movement, the feminist movement, and, currently, the fight for gay equality? To have been born before television, before the Internet, before we could traverse the earth in a day? To say what we wore, what we did to amuse ourselves, what made us sad, what made us happy. What changes over time altered how we viewed the world and ourselves?

It has been said that we do not remember days or weeks or years. We remember moments. The moment we first heard our newborn child cry. Our first kiss. Our first day at school. That short walk across the stage to receive one's high school diploma. Turning to see your soon-to-be bride walking down the aisle toward you. News sadly delivered of a child or spouse missing in action or lost on some far battlefield. These are the moments we can memorialize. These are the times we can share and pass on.

To echo a long-running daytime soap opera: these are the moments of our lives. Your life counts for something. Write it down. The future will thank you for it.

DANA BERRY'S STORIES

Dana Berry is a sunny Oregonian who grew up on the waterfront of Lake Oswego, a suburb of Portland, Oregon. She shares her love of life with audiences who deeply appreciate her wit and candid characterizations of daily life. Her work is filled with heart and humor while capturing the subtle essence of human sentiment. She genuinely and convincingly writes from a real-world life philosophy of love and gratitude, evidenced in her joyful spirit, and exposing the sweet and funny in some of life's most bitter, yet precious moments. A rustic home in the country is Dana's sanctuary, where she digs not only dirt, but joy, humor, friends, family, animals, spirituality, story sharing, and real-world issues while roasting "peeps" over a fire for s'mores.

Motherhood and Other Disasters: Halloween and Potty Talk

By Dana Berry

HALLOWEEN:

GUS HAD JUST TURNED ONE YEAR OLD. MADISON WAS TWO AND a half. I don't remember what Madison's costume was that year, but Gus was a cowboy. Since he was so young and barely walking, we bundled him up in a western blanket, strapped on his cowboy hat, popped a binky in his mouth, and pulled him around the neighborhood in his red flyer wagon.

We were living in Portland Heights where the streets were narrow, windy and hilly. They were also dark and lined with cars on both side. Since there were no sidewalks in this particular area, we had to walk in the middle of the road located behind our house. It was raining, cold, really dark, and very hard to see. A typical Portland Halloween night. The kids were doing great. Madison was scoring at each house and Gus hadn't made a peep.

By the time we got to the fourth house, I looked to see if Gus was sleeping or just taking it all in. It was hard to see much in the dark, so I had to lean in close. When I got down to where I could see his face, I noticed he was gone. He was not in the wagon. I let out a yell and began running back toward the house as fast as I could go, looking for him along the way. As I approached our driveway I spotted him in the middle of the street. Apparently, the road we were walking on was steeper than we realized and poor baby Gus had simply slipped out of the back of the wagon. He was lying on his back, wide awake, sucking on his binky, in the middle of the dark street, still wearing his hat, boots and his smile.

POTTY TALK:

I had just put the kids in their highchairs for dinner. Then I went back to the kitchen to get the meal I had prepared, carried it over to the table and set it down in front of two-year-old Madison, who took one look and said "What the hell is that?"

It took every fiber in my body to not break out into laughter. But, I knew I could not let her see me laugh, and I also knew I had to do something. But what? I thought for a quite a while, as it took me a long time to regain my composure. Finally, I said, "Madison, that kind of language is not nice to use."

"Why not, mommy?" She asked in complete innocence.

"Well, because that kind of language is called potty talk," I told her.

"Why mommy?" She asked.

"Well," I said, "because that kind of language should only be said in a bathroom so not one hears it or get their feelings hurt.

"Okay, mommy." She said.

That sure went well, I thought, for being so spur of the moment.

The next day I happened to walk by the bathroom and

heard Madison talking. I peeked my head in and saw her sitting on her little potty chair, posing as many questions as she could.

"What the hell is that?"

"What the hell is going on?"

"Who the hell are you?"

"Why the hell are you doing that?" And, so on.

For several days, she sat on her little potty chair happily swinging her legs while swearing up a storm.

Motherhood and Other Disasters: Christmas

By Dana Berry

CHRISTMAS 1993:

L ATE ONE NIGHT, IN HOPES OF AVOIDING THE CHRISTMAS RUSH, I found myself having an argument with my husband in the middle of an aisle at Toys-R-Us.

We lived in a gated community of a dozen homes on acreage. The gate was located at the top of a steep hill that wound down to where all but two of the homes were situated around a huge figure-eight-shaped road. One complete loop of the figure eight was half a mile long, making it perfect for kids to bike, skate, kick balls, and run around without much concern. So we thought one of those cool little two-seater cars would be really fun for the kids to putt around in.

As we inspected the features of each car, we agreed on a jeep that seemed perfect for our son and daughter. Plus, it was one of the only vehicles that you could get with seat belts for just twenty-five dollars more. Then I noticed there was one more option available. For an additional one hundred dollars, a roll bar could be added. This is when the argument began.

My husband believed the jeep was plenty safe with or without seat belts. His point was that the jeep weighed more than one-hundred pounds, which was more than the weight of the kids put together. How could two little kids possibly roll something that heavy and sturdy that only moves a few miles an hour? To him it didn't make any sense to spend the extra money on something that would never happen. While I could see his side of the argument, I felt better knowing that the kids, perhaps a bit young for such a toy, would be in a vehicle with every safety option available.

In the midst of the holiday atmosphere, festive music, and families in line for photos with Santa, our dialogue about a kiddy car digressed into ridiculous automotive quips pertaining to our collision-bound marriage:

"Can you just cool your engine?"

"Stop looking in the rearview mirror!"

"You really think a newer model is less maintenance."

"You need to pull your head out of your trunk."

Once we finally pulled ourselves together, I left the store embarrassed, but with a really cute red and gray jeep complete with seat belts and a roll bar.

On Christmas morning, the kids were more than ecstatic to follow the clues of our annual Christmas scavenger hunt for the big present. Upon solving and locating all the hints they finally discovered their shiny new jeep with a huge red bow wrapped around the roll bar. Within moments, we were all outside in our pajamas, winter coats and mittens learning how to drive the jeep in the skiff of snow that had fallen in the night. The kids quickly got the hang of the jeep's gear shift as they practiced going from reverse to first, second, and third. Then off they went making circles around the figure eight with smiles that lit up the still dark morning.

As the kids gained confidence behind the wheel, they

asked if they could drive to their friends' house, up by the gate, to show off their new car. It made me a bit nervous, but I didn't want to be a bah humbug mom on Christmas morning, so I reluctantly agreed with their dad, and up the hill they went. Madison was proudly behind the wheel and Gus was giddy as ever as they took off on their adventure.

The road was steep, paved and plenty wide for two cars. However, as it rose in elevation, the sides of the road became more cliff-like where the properties below had been carved out of the hillside to allow for level yards. This meant that, as you approached the top of the road, it was a good twenty-five or thirty-foot steep slope down either side.

The kids were doing great and having a blast as they stayed in the middle of the road and began their ascent. As they climbed further up the hill we noticed the car beginning to strain, and the kids began asking why they were slowing down when they had the gas pedal pressed all the way. Their dad shouted at them to "Put it in first." When the kids looked to the gear shift they slowly began veering to the side. "Keep an eye on the road" I hollered. The kids yelled back at their dad, "First or Reverse?" Then it happened. They popped the gear shift into reverse with the gas pedal still pressed to the floor and faster than we could yell "Stop" we watched them quickly hurtle backwards over the side of the road as they tumbled and rolled bumper to bumper several times down the steep embankment.

When the jeep finally came to a stop, it was upside down on its roll bar at the bottom of the embankment. Madison was thrown from the car and was sprawled out in the neighbor's yard. Gus was nowhere to be seen. We ran as fast as we could and found him still inside the jeep being held upside down in his seat belt. He was covered in dirt and had blood running down his face from a pretty good gash above his eyebrow. Madison was also covered in dirt, but completely fine. We probably should have taken Gus in for a couple stitches, but it was

Christmas, and I had some butterfly band-aids that seemed to work fine. Other than the scar above Gus's eyebrow, both kids survived that Christmas morning. Besides, they love sharing the story about the time they rolled a jeep they were driving over a cliff when they were only three and four years old.

Motherhood and Other Disasters: Summer Break

By Dana Berry

SUMMER BREAK:

A S MY KIDS APPROACHED THE COMPLETION OF ANOTHER YEAR OF school, I was desperately trying to figure out how to keep them busy for three months of summer.

Previous years had been filled with tennis lessons, soccer and basketball camps, swim lessons, visits to grandparents, a short vacation here or there to places like Lake Tahoe, San Diego, or the beach. We also did a few stay-cations, as we have now come to know them—to the zoo, downtown Portland, local festivals, and concerts. While most summer breaks were busy and fun, each year I felt challenged to find new and different things for the kids to participate in.

One morning, as I walked into the real estate office where I worked in town, I picked up a copy of the local newspaper sitting on the reception desk. Like most mornings, I began preparing for my day by enjoying a cup of coffee while flipping through the paper to see what was happening in the real estate world. Internet was so new in those days that we realtors still relied on newspapers, and a huge black and white catalogue, the size of a Los Angeles phone book, that was published weekly with every bit of information regarding residential and business listings in the Portland metropolitan area. Those books weighed a ton, but they were golden. Realtors stockpiled them in the trunks of our cars like winning lottery tickets.

Taking a sip of coffee, I turned the page of the newspaper and spotted the summer jackpot for my ten-year-old son, Gus. The local country club was hosting a free summer-long golf program for school-aged boys. But there were a limited number of spaces. Gus loved golfing, so I immediately picked up the phone and signed him up. What a score! I couldn't wait to tell Gus that he would be taking golf lessons with a pro and then playing the course with a foursome of boys his age. It also included lunch in the dining room, and use of the pool at the end of each day beginning the following week.

The day finally arrived. Gus was up early, with his clubs cleaned, and dressed like Arnold Palmer in slacks, a polo shirt and pullover knit vest. He was ready to play some serious golf. There were no more municipal courses in his future from where he stood that morning.

As we slowly approached the country club by way of the tree-lined road and immaculate grounds, I was thrilled to see how happy Gus was for his summer to begin. When we arrived at the clubhouse, a golf pro waved us in, opened Gus's door, welcomed him, checked him off on the list, and told me to pick him up by four o'clock. I returned to my office as happy as could be for Gus.

Around two o'clock I received a call from the country club. The man on the phone told me what a great little golfer and nice young man my son was. How kind of him to check in with me, I thought. But what he said next startled me. Apparently, the country club forgot to put the fine print in the newspaper advertising the eight free weeks of golf for young boys. In hopes of increasing their membership they were only offering this special deal to people who had toured the club and made a deposit toward becoming a new member. Somehow when I called to sign Gus up we were put on that list without any questions.

After I dropped Gus off someone in the business department noticed that I had not yet made my ten-thousand-dollar deposit as the now more serious man ask if I could bring that in when I came to pick up Gus in two hours. I explained that I was not interested in a country club membership at this time, and proceeded to beg him to please let Gus stay as it was obviously not my mistake. The man was relentless. Gus could only stay if I paid ten thousand dollars. He wheezed heavily into the phone. My heart sank deep knowing how disappointed my son was no doubt going to be.

Once again, driving up that beautiful tree-lined road to the clubhouse, I could see Gus. He and some of the other boys were lounging on the pool terrace, eating sandwiches, cookies and drinks with umbrellas in the bright sunshine. When Gus spied me approaching, he lifted his drink toward me with a smile that wouldn't stop as the pool water reflected across his browning skin and white teeth. He was in his element. In his mind, he was not just drinking an Arnold Palmer, he was Arnold Palmer.

Gus got in the car and immediately began telling me all about his dream day while I avoided the scrutinizing looks of the staff when they saw Gus toss his clubs on top of the two-hundred real estate books in the trunk of my car. Gus talked about his amazing day the entire drive home while I rehearsed how I would break the news to him.

When we pulled into the garage I told him that I needed to tell him something. He sat there and took it like a man. I could tell he was heartbroken, but somehow he kept smiling as I shared the bad news. It was a bit confusing. When I was done, I apologized and asked if he was okay. He said he understood and then asked, "So, Mom, are you saying that I basically crashed a private country club for the whole day?" I smiled and told him that he could look at it that way. With that he smiled as big as when I picked him up just twenty minutes earlier and said, "Cool! That's even better. I can't wait to tell all my friends I crashed a private country club for a whole day without getting caught."

It was amazing to witness my ten-year-old boy turn such bad news into a win for himself that day. Twenty years later Gus still beams when he tells the story of his best ever summer vacation.

LISA DE BRITAIN'S STORIES

Lisa de Britain worked as a reading and language acquisition educator for many years. She now enjoys retirement in Portland, Oregon. She determinedly tussles with the mysterious practice of writing, the mental exercise of learning Italian, and the joy of sharing her life with Sadie, her Newfoundland Landseer service dog, also retired.

I See: Vision and Sight

By Elizabeth de Britain

"**I** SEE."

I often use this simple sentence now to indicate understanding or agreement. I use "I see" as a verbal nod, or as a refined "uh-huh" or "gotcha." With "I see," I imply that "I'm still here. I'm still following what you say." But I don't see. Not really. Mind you, for more than sixty years, I didn't know that I didn't see. At least I didn't see what you would have seen, but I didn't know that. Even now, you would need to understand what to look for to see my dilemma. The issues, you see, are with my brain, not my eyes. "Hmm, now I see."

In February 2006, after surgery to repair a congenital Chiari malformation at the base juncture of my skull and central nervous system, the doctors found that I had significant developmental brain damage. This should have precluded a lifetime of reading, some forms of manual dexterity, normal mobility, and visual activities generally. I tried and finally limped away from tap dancing and gymnastics, bruised and embarrassed. As life became more complex, the brain fatigue continued to increase, and so I frequently napped. I slept in odd places and at odd times, too weary to get to my bed. I stumbled around college campuses for years, somehow managing without serious accommodation. My eyes were busy, just not efficient. This required that my brain work much faster in order to compensate.

And yet, by pure happenstance, my advanced studies were in managing undiagnosed learning disabilities impacting children's reading and language acquisition. I taught the children to read, even though I shouldn't have been able to read myself. "Oh," I nodded, not quite convinced. "I see."

Vision is not the process I thought it was. The eyes do not see something and then inform the brain of what they see. Rather, the brain decides what it needs and tells the eyes what to go look for. Then the eyes team up together and set off on the search. They follow the directive to match that mental image with the outside world.

This is why, without specific concentrated mental effort, if we are already late to pick up our offspring from soccer practice and get them to their basketball game, we can't find our keys. This is even more true if the search is accompanied by verbalizations running along the lines of "Why can't we ever just . . . ?" Or "Where the hell are those keys?" We overload our brains, brains so distracted they can't form the complete mental image for our eyes to search out. We occupy valuable brain time and space with thoughts of cars, kids, soccer, time, guilt, amount of gas in the gas tank, and perhaps the wholesome home-cooked meal versus take-out for the third-time-this-week dilemma. All this means that our brains aren't getting the message through to our eyes accurately. So our eyes gaze around, *literally mindlessly*, looking at nothing in particular, until we stop, focus, and let our brains concentrate specifically on what our keys look like and where they are likely to be. Then, there they are, right where we left them.

However, my brain didn't, and still doesn't, transmit requests normally. Instead, each eye receives instructions independently of the other. And then, instead of doing a visual mind-meld, my eyes squabble with one another. They do not team. Instead, they return two separate observations to the brain for decoding and discussion. Sometimes this shows up as double vision. Sometimes, one eye shuts down, but not always the same eye. This requires yet another brain-based committee meeting for updating, prioritizing, and decision-making. This laborious series of activities has continued constantly whenever my eyes have been open during my entire lifetime. I was at least sixty years old before I knew that. And that explains a lot. "Of course. I see now."

At first, I was thrilled to finally understand why, as a child, I had been constantly boinked on the head with the tetherball, and why I never hit a softball. Why, too, I fell down stairs, even fell up stairs, stumbled over doorsills, and was generally hopeless at anything that required me to move and to think at the same time. So I concentrated on seated activities at school. Reading was arduous to master, but less painful and embarrassing than sports. I was always the last to be chosen for ball teams, but I was reasonably popular when it came to math, spelling bees, and later, physics.

All of which was unwitting preparation for teaching learning disabled children to read. Later, I moved on to teaching adults. Throughout my life, I stumbled and staggered. Each eye worked well enough, just not together. Klutzy, but smart enough, I did what I was normally expected to do. I graduated from high school, went off to college, married, raised three children, lived abroad, divorced, and remarried, all the while knocking into walls, falling on and off ski lifts, losing everything from keys to children, and, less dramatically, making strange arrangements of furniture and flowers. Coupled with this fluctuating double vision, I had no depth perception. Oh, I knew when a house was behind a car parked at a curb. I just didn't see it. I had no sense of space or volume surrounding and between them. Last year, I finally saw in three dimensions. The first time I saw "fat trees"—one behind another—I nearly drove off the road.

I still work with a wonderful neuro-optometrist and a dedicated vision therapist. I wear glasses with heavy-duty prisms that help to team my eyes. Over the last year, we have taught the muscles to try to cooperate. Most days I have some depth perception. My brain and my eyes are developing cooperating skill sets. We have come a long way. It is slow and difficult work.

Meanwhile, while I worked on adapting my brain and eye coordination, miraculous adaptive advancements have been developed. For me, the greatest by far is my Kindle—my three Kindles, actually. In exchange for these magical machines, I have happily traded entire rooms filled with books that are too fatiguing to read or even to find some days. Now I have hundreds, maybe a thousand books at my fingertips, not to mention entire libraries of rented books. Not only can I now adjust the background brightness, spacing, and font size, but I can read text-to-speech and audio books when I am simply too tired to read visually. And still, I read—three or four books a week. I regularly read the *New York Times*, the *Washington Post*, Reuters, AP, the *Guardian*, the *Economist*, and countless journals and magazines. I do still have one bookcase with reference books and DYI manuals, filled mostly with pictures. And I do still keep cookbooks, though mostly as a catalogue of past culinary glories.

It is in my beloved book club that the reality of vision loss has become more than my personal issue. I weep for the struggle of my friends. Cataracts, glaucoma, macular degeneration, diabetic retinopathy—the effects of aging have been devastating. Only a few in our book club can still read hardback books easily now. And only two still determinedly prefer to read traditional books, albeit published in large print. Fifteen years ago, the rest of us would no longer be reading at all. Still, for us, for our book club, the companionship is far more important than the conversation over book versus electronic device. Instead, we congratulate ourselves on our ability to continue being attached to the world by whatever means necessary. Our group is a miracle, you see. That we can see to read is another miracle. Accommodation is not capitulation. It is only a tool to better understand a remarkable world. I see.

Notes to a New Dog in the Neighborhood

By Sadie de Britain (Transcribed by Elizabeth de Britain)

WELCOME TO THE NEIGHBORHOOD, GINGER!
I hope you remember me from the dog park yesterday. I'm Sadie, the big black and white border collie/Newfoundland mix. You said that you had just adopted the family on the corner. Well done! The ones with grey hair and glasses are excellent choices. They are two of my very favorite people. But (and with humans there is always a "but") they come without owners' manuals, which, if you will allow me to say so, is wildly inefficient. Even when they were young and still operated smoothly, both our families had their tricky quirks. Now they are called "issues." If you add on decades and decades and decades of wear and tear, boy, they are really complicated to keep humming along in the right lane. So here are ten tips to make things a bit easier:

1. They like perky, as in ears, but not too much bouncing.

Vertical movement and a lot of noise only confuses humans, and then they bark.

2. They like perky eyes. Again, easy does it. Staring at them in that certain tone of voice and shouting "Look, look!" at every squirrel, bird, or falling leaf just wears them out, and then they need naps.

3. About naps: you'll get a lot of these, because *they* need a lot of these. Think of naps as crowd control. At least when they are napping, you know where they are and that they aren't getting into too much trouble.

4. Trouble. For humans, there are only three types of trouble you need to worry about: other people, your noise and their stuff.

5. They worry a lot about what other people think. Most people have enough to worry about in their own lives without paying much attention to yours. Still, when other humans are around, look good, stay calm and, please, no jumping (refer to Tip #1).

6. To them, your enthusiastic barking is noise. And for them noise doesn't mean "Wow, will you look at that! Isn't that interesting? Let's go check it out!" For our families it means, "Now what? Wait a minute, wait a minute. Gotta get out of this chair first." So use noise judiciously.

7. And their stuff. They have lots and lots of stuff. They like their stuff just where it is, unless they've put it someplace where it doesn't belong. Then they begin to bark. Anyway, don't move their stuff. They like their stuff just as it is. So don't chew on it, piddle on it, or leave delicious smells on it, even though you would no doubt be improving it.

8. Get used to calmly going about your own business when, for

no good reason, they will swoop you up and hug the living bejesus out of you. Warning: soon, their friends will too. And smooching. Strangers smooching your ears. Lord, save us!

9. Speaking of The Lord, humans aren't known for their spelling or their capacity for big-picture thinking. We even gave them the clue about God by spelling it backwards . . . and they still don't get it. So be on your best behavior and show them how they are supposed to act. Just love them a lot, be patient, and put up with all their weirdnesses. If they are having a bad day, you can always suggest a walk or a treat. It's good for them and for you.

10. Catch them doing something right. You are in charge, so lead. Lots of positive reinforcement. Don't get mad or even discouraged. They really are doing the best they can, even if it isn't always cute. Two things are sure. They will soon want a nap, and they will almost always want to hug, to smooch, and generally love you to bits. And that's what you are here for, to teach them how to love and how to be loveable. That's really all there is to it.

Chow.
Your new friend,
Sadie

P.S. Forget the owners' manuals. Manuals are all about leash laws and puppy training. Rubbish. It is our families that need to be on leashes . . . and they are certainly the ones who need the training. Still, you have made great strides with yours in just a couple of weeks. Naps and love. Naps and love. Just lead by example. Good luck!

Mr. Zavros's Newspaper

By Elizabeth de Britain

L AST NIGHT, AFTER ANOTHER DISTURBING TELEVISION NEWSCAST, I recalled a very ordinary Wednesday afternoon in November of 2001. I was the director of the ESL (English as a Second Language) center on a large college campus less than seven miles from where one of the planes had tragically struck the Pentagon just a few weeks before. That afternoon, two grim government agents—one from the FBI and one from the CIA—were waiting in my office when I arrived. They came under the Patriot Act mandate. They had been there before. They would come again.

Their interest in our hundreds of new English language learners worried our staff and our students. My guests insisted that we were to very methodically review, re-vet, watch, and report on all our students. They were to have access to these students' files without cause or permission. I nervously reminded them that my job was teaching, not surveillance. Up to this point, they had not forced the issue. They had dealt directly with me and had not approached our students. But we were all very skittish. We had been watching the news, reading the newspapers and speculating amongst ourselves.

Every one of our students knew whom our visitors were and why they were there. Most of our students were new immigrants; many were either refugees, green-card holders or temporary foreign workers. Many held F-1 visas, allowing them to study in American universities. Many others were new U.S. citizens. The truth was that we had been wary of any questionable documentation for years. Occurrences such as these had been common enough in their homelands. The news of our visitors would spread quickly. I worried about empty chairs in silent classrooms if students stayed away from the danger, because their fears were not unfounded.

With some trepidation, I approached my classroom that evening. But there was Mr. Zavros, already in his usual seat and engrossed in his newspaper. We shared a long, distressed look with one another. Then he smiled slightly, rose, nodded, and settled back into his reading. Mr. Zavros was a small Greek man in his late 60s, carefully dressed in a very old coat and tie and carrying his books, newspaper, and supper in a battered briefcase. He took his studies very seriously. They all did.

By 6:40, only one seat was empty. I had forgotten about the extraordinary courage and persistence that immigrants develop. It was a Wednesday. On Wednesdays, my students were required to bring a copy of any current English language newspaper to class. Their choices told me a lot about their ambitions and their heady expectations for their language skills. Some brought the *Washington Post*, of course, and some the local community paper. And if they had commuted by public transport, they recycled parts of the *Wall Street Journal*, the *New York Times* and other area newspapers left behind by fellow travelers.

All students began silently reading any articles of interest. Then they discussed what they read with nearby students. This led to lively conversations and differing opinions based on their sources and prior knowledge. Reports of football/ soccer matches were favorite topics. Even the exchange of recipes could be part of the conversation. Of particular interest was any reference to events in their home countries. Towards the end of that evening's sharing, they touched carefully on what they knew or didn't understand about what was happening here in Virginia. The essential question: Where could they go to get reliable information?

I called for questions or observations about the process of reading newspapers. One question brought me up short: "Why do the newspapers write about the same thing but report it so differently?" I had never considered this to be unusual. But they did. For some of them, their experience was limited to the government-endorsed news sources in their homelands. Those papers proved more of a point of departure for speculation, rumor and hearsay than as reliable sources of information. For this reason, my students were confused by not just the differences between our papers, but within a single paper as well. How could this be? What is the truth? What should they believe?

I smiled and set aside my lesson plan. Thus began a long evening of dissecting an ordinary American newspaper. In English. We began at the top of the front page; it was important to choose the right paper to get the information they sought. So, what did the banner tell the reader? They decided that they could expect the *Wall Street Journal* to focus on the national and international financial news. *Leesburg Today* would be useful for finding their children's soccer scores, but they would need a national newspaper such as the *New York Times* for news from home. Imagine—choices of newspapers!

We talked about a story being "above the fold," why the far right-hand column on the front page carried the most important story, based on the editorial bias of the newspaper. What was editorial bias? What did the font size say about an article? They loved this. They eagerly searched for the "buried" news on the inside pages below the crease. They were thrilled to find where the somewhat dubious, or at least speculative reporting, would be printed. We talked about bylines and news agencies such as Reuters, The Associated Press, and United Press International. They began to learn how to separate editorials and opinions from factual reporting. All this in English! It wasn't perfect English, but their need to understand and to be understood pushed them beyond our usual grammar lessons.

Two hours later, we looked at the responsibility of the reader. This was puzzling. Most of the students were intrigued with American freedom of speech. The responsibility to thoughtfully consider what was said or written and to come to an independent conclusion as a reader confused them. From this came the issue of reliable multiple sourcing and prior knowledge.

Another hour flew by. They questioned and answered amongst themselves in the only language they had in common—English. Well past our usual release time, I asked the students whether this had been a productive use of their precious time and money. All the tired faces grinned. They had used their new language to grapple with abstract ideas, unexpected challenges of a democracy and public discourse. I was delighted with the class, making mental notes that we needed to work on the subjunctive case, the past and future perfect tenses. Mostly, I just grinned too. This type of response even from the most dedicated students is not always typical.

But it was Mr. Zavros who captured the sense of the evening best. He raised his hand. I nodded. He stood up and bowed slightly. "Tonight, Mrs. Teacher," he said. "You have made me a man now." Silence filled the room. Then he continued. "In my country, men gather each day to think together. It is our job to read, to understand, to decide. The safety of our people depends on us. But no one has asked me what I thought since I left my home. Here, people tell me what to do. I think they don't care what I think. And in my hurry for life in America, I forgot. Tonight, I feel like a man again." Mr. Zavros nodded just a bit and quietly sat down.

Memoir and Designing a Life

By Lisa de Britain

ON THAT SUNDAY IN JANUARY, I SHOULD HAVE BEEN WRITING the first draft of a memoir for Tuesday's writing group. Instead, I was watching a TED talk on YouTube, still, arguably, a worthwhile activity. More about that in a moment.

I have been in somewhat of a quandary regarding memoir writing for years. Memoir writing is essentially assembling a personal history on a timeline with reasonable accuracy. Good grammar and spelling are useful. Humor is also welcome. So why bother writing a memoir if it is essentially just a private historic reflection? Like most people, I had originally planned to use my memoir to tell my family how they came to end up right here in this, their lives. I'd tell them how hard other people had worked and sacrificed to secure that place for them. Success or failure, it was the struggle, the hope for the future, and the sheer grit of the efforts of strangers out of their past that resulted in the world my children and their children inherited. At the very least, I thought I might finally get the last word in about the family, *the real story*, the true story. After all, I would be the one writing it down, and that goes a long way towards making my story the official one.

The TED talk in question was called "Designing a Life." The topic stunned me. Designing a life? Not living a life. Not joyfully managing, planning, funding, organizing, or transforming a life, or even squandering, rebelling from, or waiting for a life. Designing . . . a life.

Designing is an interesting concept in itself. Designing suggests the active, intentional development of something unfinished and intrinsically unique. Inherent in designing something new is change itself. It has to do with the setting of priorities, reviewing of choices, and forestalling the expectation of an easy conclusion. And it usually carries with it risk, false starts, and the opportunity to begin again and again. So designing a life would always be a work in progress. Certainly it would involve uncertainty.

So why take on redesigning a life for the future while writing a memoir about the past my family doesn't even know? Why now, in my mid-70s? How would that work?

These "why" questions about memoir and designing a life are not rhetorical. I have thought about them for some time. I could find only one convincing answer to the question, "Why a memoir, now, to buttress the rest of my life?" The answer— simply because I can. For the first time in my life, I can. There is no long list of obligations and relationships that take precedence. There are no pressing mandates. I am alone now to set my own course, albeit one more limited than I would wish. It is mine to navigate. A vision of a great flat white space surrounds me. Gone are the rocky horizons—years of marriage, divorce, hope and disappointment, another marriage, another divorce, childrearing, illness, death, career, and repeated moves across town, across country, across continents. My prospects now look far less cluttered, but more intense and closer at hand. Perhaps memoir and recrafting my life could work in tandem. Reflection on the past as the basis for realigning my life now—would that work? My life history actively interwoven into my future life? Could I construct meaning from my own history?

Perhaps, I can. For one thing, the long lens of history defines not only events but also the values and ethics surrounding them. Over time, some people, places and things show themselves to have been of greater or of longer lasting value than others. It is true for most of us, I think, even my people, the Adams family. For good or ill, my relatives instilled their principles in me when I was a child. These formed the basis for most of a lifetime of decisions. Now, they reassert themselves again, particularly in unfamiliar, trying, or frightening situations. Events and other relationships further formed my values. Some of these have been long forgotten. Yet they show in what I have carried with me through my life. So what did I hang on to, and what did I jettison, and why? How do those values and experiences continue to influence me today, and going forward?

In the telling of the stories, I hope to uncover new insights into who I have been and who I might choose to become. Just because I can.

SAM BRUNO'S STORY

Sam Bruno, age 84, was born in San Jose, California, formerly the Garden City, now known as Silicon Valley. After dropping out of college, he ventured to Hollywood, chasing an improbable dream. He is a retired AT&T Pacific Bell Yellow Pages advertising salesman, and has lived in Lake Oswego for the past thirteen years. He has enjoyed running, hiking, walking, fishing (both fly and deep sea), thoroughbred racing, movies, reading, and now memoir writing. He would like to give special thanks to Ron Talney, who, by example, created a safe place for him to share and better understand his part in the play. He sends huge hugs to his wife Marilyn for putting up with a "dinosaur" who can't even turn on a computer. And finally, without the generous assistance of Louise Mengelkoch, this ship would never have sailed!

The Carpenter's Son and Shoeshine Memories

By Sam Bruno

SANTA CLARA—SAN JOSE, CALIFORNIA, 1985

DRIVING PAST THE SANTA CLARA CATHOLIC CEMETERY, I AM overcome with love, anger, grief, loss, guilt, fear, and memories, as my mind races back forty years in time. Now I am twelve years old, dancing the tarantella at the SES Portuguese Hall just down the street with Aunt Marguerite to the music of Cousin Ralph the drummer and his band, "The Ravioli Destroyers." The band is keeping all the Paisanos hopping, swinging, swaying, hugging, and kissing late into the night. Enjoying vino and highballs and meatballs and spaghetti and sausages. The antipasto table overflows with Italian delicacies.

Now, in the present, I'm driving through the main entrance past the rows of mausoleums, beautifully maintained green lawns and flower gardens. Finally, after several frustrating right turns, left turns, U-turns at the corner of a lane of modest tombstones, at last I arrive. It's Mom's and Dad's gravesite—a double vault stacked one on the bottom where Dad has been since his death in 1967, one on the top that will entomb my mom when it's her time. The gravestone has our family name on top. Sam's photo is on the left (1908-1967). On the right is Mary's (1909-19__).

I am living in the present and the past as if stepping in and out of a time machine like Alley Oop, the newspaper comics character I read in the *San Jose Evening News* during my childhood and adolescence. The SES Hall with all the celebrations on all the festive occasions of the past with relatives and friends, just minutes from here. Now, so many years later, in midlife, I'm here at the cemetery on a mission of redemption, forgiveness, and amends with my deceased father and the ghosts of memories with those same loved ones and friends now entombed here in death but alive in spirit. The moment, the experience, is beyond overwhelming—so filled with emotion!

Dropping to my knees on the lawn in front of his headstone, tears flowing, feeling my heart beating, crying in a confused emotional abyss, with mind and heart searching for the words, a magical thought and feeling came to me. KEEP IT SIMPLE! "Dad, I'm sorry! At this moment I love you more than ever! <u>PLEASE FORGIVE ME</u> because I have total, unconditional love and forgiveness in my heart for you!!!

Several weeks later, running on Aptos Beach, as I had done for many years (sometimes in deep meditation), through the Esplanade, past the Rio Beach Store and Pixie's Market, heading south, with the PG&E smokestack barely visible in miniature (fifteen miles away at Moss Landing), a voice spoke to me, aided by the afternoon breeze off the Pacific. It was clear, and so was the vision. It was my father running behind me desperately trying to keep up, saying "Sammy, Sammy, I'm sorry. I love you! Forgive me! I forgive you! Wait, slow down, please, wait for me!" Overwhelmed, I stared back as the vision of Dad and the sound of his voice faded away on the wind until it/he was gone—stored away with the memories of my life.

Thirty years later, he still appears, with no advance reason or occasion. There he will be with me on "The Cement Boat" at Aptos, fishing with me. I am nine years old and have a rubber-lipped surf perch on my line. His favorite place to haunt me is at the horse races, studying the racing form and handicapping until the wee hours of the night. During my Hollywood starving actor years, the highlight of his life was to visit me while I worked the tracks of Hollywood Park and Santa Anita, then eating pasta and meatballs at Joe's Little Italy in downtown L.A., schmoozing with some of my drop-dead gorgeous actress friends. Ah, bittersweet dreams of Dad and pasta, racing forms—the morning line, post time, and good red wine. Now, only in my dreams . . .

SAN JOSE, LATE SUMMER 1943

Remembering more. Dad was busy in his garage workshop. I could hear the sounds of wood being sawed and the hammering of nails. Smoke came from the metal chimney vent on the roof of the shop. When that chimney was smoking, Dad would always be working in there. Especially in cold weather, he would be enjoying his antique cast-iron railroad stove. Not far from our house was the Southern Pacific roundhouse, where the big train engines were repaired, steam-cleaned and serviced. My dad had a friend who worked there. When their small upright cast-iron stove was replaced with a big potbelly, the old stove was given to him and he passed it on to my dad. That old beauty really heated up the shop.

"Whatcha doing, Pop?" I asked.

"I'm making a shoeshine box for you. I noticed you made some good tips over the holidays shining shoes for your uncles and friends, even with your polish and brushes in a plain paper bag. You should have a real shoe-shine box! Saturday we're going to the roller rink and see how you do with the servicemen. They always need their shoes shined!"

"What'll I charge 'em, Pop?"

"Fifteen cents," Pop said. "Know why?"

"No Pop. Why?"

"Cuz they'll flip you a quarter and many of the guys will say 'KEEP THE CHANGE, KID.'" That shoeshine box has been part of my life for seventy years, ever since my father made it for me so long ago. It was painted green and had a simple design—an open box bottom with the two larger ends pyramiding up about fifteen inches with a wood shoe footprint on top, where my customers placed their feet when I shined. I carved a big 15¢ on one end. Thru the years, the box, with its crude design and fading paint, has been important to me. It symbolized many of my life's phases and emotions, childhood and adolescence, earning money, being thrifty, socializing with people, years of loyalty, and longevity. I see my own life's journey—worthwhile, enduring, fulfilling and a life well-lived and with purpose in that box. We're both still here!

So, the next Saturday afternoon, in San Jose, where the El Camino Real and a street called the Alameda made a sweeping turn past Tiny's Drive-In, The Town Motel, the Rio Nido Mexican Restaurant, and the Singing Barber Shop, I picked a spot for myself and my green shoeshine box at the entrance of the roller rink. I began shining shoes of the soldiers, sailors, marines and Seabees who were all going skating, having a Coca Cola and a hot dog, and flirting with the pretty girls. The music blared from the speakers, playing Glenn Miller's "In the Mood," Johnny Mercer's "Pardon Me Boys, is That the Chattanooga Choo-Choo?" (Track 29 – "Boy, can you give me a shine?") And shine I did!

Sometimes I would sneak in the entrance where they were taking shoes off and putting on rented skates, leaving the shoes on shelves while they skated. I would quickly shine those shoes, with permission or not, and then hang around and hustle the guys for tips. (These would be the guys I had missed when they were coming in the door.)

Business was usually good, sometimes VERY GOOD, depending on whether I knew the guy working the room where the skates were stored, or not so good when I got kicked out to the street, back to where I started!

When I got home, a few blocks from the rink, I emptied my shoebox of nickels, dimes, quarters, and half-dollars (they were used in the 40s), and occasionally a one-dollar bill! Depending on the crowd, I could haul in two to four bucks, occasionally nine to ten dollars and once twelve dollars!!

How did I do it? Well, these servicemen, and very occasionally a WAC or a WAVE, usually had just finished basic training at Fort Ord in Monterey, sixty-five miles south of San Jose. They were killing time until they took the train from the Southern Pacific Depot, just a few blocks from the rink, to board troop ships at Alameda, Oakland, or San Francisco, just fifty miles north. They were going to the WAR!

Sadly though, history tells me that many of the servicemen whose shoes I shined gave their lives at Normandy, Berlin, Stalingrad, the Pacific and many of the other battlefields for the cause of freedom. Back then San Jose was called "The Garden City," with about a dozen canneries—Murison Label, Continental Can, American Can Co. and other businesses related to the fruit and vegetable canning industry that ran 24/7. And now, with the astonishing emergence of the Silicon Valley technology revolution, not a tree or vine is left. Nothing anyone could eat grows there anymore!

Epilogue: As this old grey-haired curmudgeon reflects back to a simpler time, when life and work were mostly hands-on, human labor skills were necessary. Me, I'll be just a fleeting memory. My life has been for the most part, as good, or not as good, as I let it be. My serious concern is for the younger generations. Where will they fit in? Will robots shine shoes? (haha) It's a solid bet that these 20-something logarithm geniuses never even noticed when the last prune tree disappeared from Silicon Valley. They obviously never heard about the last man who cut down the last tree on Easter Island.

SHARYN INZUNZA'S STORY

Sharyn Inzunza writes marketing content for a living. And to help with the creative side of her work, she writes stories, often about growing up in rural Australia. She meets with her memoir-writing group each Tuesday, where she shares a new tale with her wonderful story-telling friends, then heads back to her work, refreshed and inspired for another week.

A Feast of Pig Parts and Italians

By Sharyn Inzunza

It's the late 1990s, and we're living on a goat farm on the Mediterranean island of Sardinia. The farm sits between the ancient towns of Arzachena and Cannigione. These Italian communities burst with tourists in the summer. But come winter, frigid winds blow the landscape clean of all but the locals and us, the foreigners. The Sardo residents, carved from the granite landscape, tolerate us outsiders with stony indifference.

Unless, of course, there's a feast.

We live in a sprawling stone farmhouse—a patchwork of tiled rooms that branch off from a long, windowless hallway. In the warm months, we fling the rooms' shutters and windows wide open and inhale the beauty of grapevines heavy with fruit and the earthy aroma of ambivalent sheep, their rhythmic lips tugging at the grasses. In the winter, as the cold seeps through the thick stone walls, we wear gloves and hats to bed. And when the fierce *Mistrale* winds escape from northern Africa, the faithful shutters rattle and whistle against the violent foe.

And at the back of our house, sheep huddle together in a mono-fleece, their faces buried against the wind's frigid sting.

In town, storefronts disappear behind metal garage doors, leaving only a skeleton of businesses open for the locals. *Arzachenans* and *Canningoneons*, wrapped in heavy wool coats and scarves, click along the frigid streets on wooden legs. The icy winds sweep our memories clean of *gelati* on the piazza and strolls through the narrow cobblestone streets. And scrubby pines cling to the thin earth, their wiry tufts elongated from a lifetime of windy abuse.

And when I drive into town to buy bread from the *panificio*, produce from the indoor *mercato* or grab a quick *caffe* from the smoky corner bar, my interaction with the locals is bleak, like the landscape, limited to *buon giorno* and *grazie*.

My landlord's daughter Antonella speaks English. She is the liaison between us and her parents, Isabella and Francesco. They built the farmhouse that we rent for their retirement. But they felt lost in the hollow rooms, so they remained in their cozy house in the small town of San Pantaleo. However, they visit the farm every day. Francesco milks the goat (and drinks a glass of the still-warm milk) and Isabella processes the remaining milk into cheese. Underneath the house is a full basement. Here they make their sweet wine and Sardo-style cheeses. The space resembles a mini-factory with large vats and other equipment lurking in the shadows of the damp space.

The front third of the basement is the gathering area. There's a kitchen to the right side of the room, a long table down the middle, and laminate storage closets at the other end. The kitchen is below our bedroom. Once a year, as the air warms and the turquoise waters of the Mediterranean flirt and sparkle again, Isabella and Francesco hold a pig feast in the basement. This year, they've invited us *"gli Americani"* to join them. Preparing for the feast is a week-long affair. Antonella tells us that the men "take care of the pig," and then the women prepare it.

Several days before the feast, as I bump along the dusty driveway to the house, I see Francesco and his friends—Sardo men dressed in their earthy farm clothes and woolen flat caps. They're standing in a circle near the pig pens, some with their fists on their hips, others with relaxed hands clasped behind their backs. I get out of the car, unable to resist a glance at the bloodied carcass hanging against the pig pen's white wall. For the next several days, tiny Fiats and Ape three-wheeled cars litter the front yard. Our house echoes with the clanging of pots, pans, and assertive chatter, as the women work in the kitchen below.

On the day of the feast, in the early afternoon, the doorbell rings, echoing through the house. We come out and Isabella is standing at the gate to our courtyard wearing her floral half-apron over a cotton smock dress. *"Ciao, ciao! Prego?"* Are you ready? We follow her into the basement. As we enter the room, my cellar of Italian words dries up in my throat. Spirited conversations shrink to whispers as weathered faces turn toward the Americans. The guests, who speak in the *Arzachena* and *Cannigione* dialects, dot the perimeter of the long rustic table. They murmur *"Ciao"* and nod as Isabella introduces us.

Antonella beckons us to sit next to her. The older women anchor the kitchen end of the table, the men keep a comfortable distance at the opposite end and the young ones fill in the middle. A sheet of white paper covers the table, secured by white dinner plates. Waif-like plastic plates rest on top for the hors d'oeuvres: Sardo pâté and olives. Bottles of homemade red and white wine and loaves of crusty bread flow down the middle of the table. When we're done, the women whisk away our dishes. And the pig feast officially begins.

The ladies place large bowls of steaming pork risotto along the table, a pallid dish of creamy pork-flavored rice. They clear the bowls and present the next course. Antonella cautions ominously, "Do not feel obligated to eat anything." Oval metal platters, heavy with fragrant meat, surf the table over weathered hands. Guests dig forks into slices of blood sausage, the pig's natural casing slack and spongy around the dark meat. There are two types of blood sausage: sweet and salty. I take a slice of the salty sausage and offer the platter to Antonella. She passes it on with a *"No grazie."*

Fresh platters wobble along the table. There are organ meats. The grey-brown pig organs are whole but thinly sliced. I take a piece of liver that tastes like chalky pâté. My husband removes a slice from the tongue shape. The main course platters arrive, brimming with cuts of light and dark meat, chops, ribs and crispy rinds. Bowls of green salad balance the fatty pig parts. As the wine flows, we transition from quiet outsiders—looked upon with suspicion—to animated participants in this traditional Sardo feast. After more wine, our oil-and-vinegar languages merge and roll over our tongues.

Antonella weaves us into conversations. We laugh and my Italian vocabulary bubbles to the surface. Antonella's husband, a tall, reserved *carabinieri*, pulls my husband into the men's conversation, with frequent appeals to Antonella for help. Once the topic of *calcio* (soccer) comes up, they laugh, their faces and hands speaking a universal language.

Eventually, baskets of mandarins and apples replace the heavy meat platters, and Francesco's potent sweet wine fills small glasses. At this stage of the feast, the "aunts" test out their English on us and enhance our textbook Italian with colorful Sardo expressions. They gesture toward the men, who smile their mosaic-toothed smiles, before turning back to their conversations with shrugs and flying hands. Laughter bounces around the stone room, over the crooked stacks of metal platters and across the grease-splattered tablecloth.

Amidst the laughter and patchworked language, the women present the last course of the pig feast—a deep white bowl of chocolate pudding. It travels from guest to guest, each one scooping the cakey dessert onto their plate. I take some and pass the bowl to Antonella. She throws her hands in the air with a "No way!" gesture. "This pudding, *Sanguinaccio*," she says, "it is made from the pig's blood, chocolate and . . . whatever else they put in pudding!"

It's delicious. We laugh and continue our stories.

Leaving is difficult, like wading through molasses, the short distance to the door thick with our swaying Sardo friends. *"Mille grazie"* and the smack of *bacci* on our cheeks fill the air as we say our goodbyes. We step out into the quiet of the warm night, leaving the chatter and laughter muffled behind the amber glass door. We return to the solitude of our house through the heavy double front doors. And at our dining room table, dwarfed by the cavernous fireplace, we reflect on the evening—the wine, the pig parts and the warmth of the Sardo people.

CATHIE JACOBS'S STORIES

Cathie Jacobs was born in Portland, Oregon, in 1943 and is a resident of Lake Oswego. She received her B.A. in human studies from Marylhurst College. She loves dogs, bird watching, writing, gardening, and traveling.

The Mummy

By Cathie Jacobs

MEXICO CITY, OCTOBER 30, 1980

THE SUNRISE THAT DAY IN MEXICO CITY WAS TYPICAL. IT WAS beautiful, with hues of pinkish-brown light permeating the landscape. These dramatic sunrises were actually due to the heavy pollution blanketing the city. You could cut the diesel in the air with a knife.

My mother was arriving that day from Portland, Oregon, for an extended visit. I was excited to see her and we had plans to visit a lot of places in Mexico. I took a look around and realized I had a mountain of dishes to wash. The kids were off to school and my husband off to work. I started to tackle the kitchen mess, but I discovered there was no hot water. To reach the pilot light that fed the hot-water tank, I had to ascend an iron spiral staircase and climb two floors up.

In Mexico, houses are not heated and propane tanks are used to heat water. I reached the roof and spied the tank. The pilot light was out, just as I suspected. With matches in hand, I lit the pilot light. It didn't take, so I pumped the gas a number of times and lit it again. It still did not take, so I pumped more gas. There was no scent of gas in the air, so I lit it again. I had my head bent over, trying to see if the pilot light was not lit, when a giant explosion blew me across the flat rooftop to the other end.

I was in shock but somehow managed to checked out the damage. It had melted my nightgown, burned my arm and worst of all, blown up in my face. The explosion singed off my eyelashes, eyebrows and much of my hairline. I had the wherewithal to make it down off the roof to the living room. I called my husband. It took him three hours to arrive home, due to the horrendous local traffic. My cat and dog sat next to me the entire time, sensing something was wrong. My husband damaged the underside of his car from driving fast over topes (speed bumps) to get home. He draped my coat over me, and we went to the emergency room of the American hospital.

It was obvious to the hospital staff that I had been burned, even though there were no tell-tale signs. Burns usually show their damage a little later. They were very experienced with such burns, for propane explosions were common in Mexico City. The doctor slathered my face and arm with colloidal silver and wrapped me in gauze, leaving holes for only my mouth and nose. I was "mummy extraordinaire." I would have to return every day to have the bandages changed. My husband had prepared my mother for my condition, but, even so, she was visibly shaken. My lips were so swollen that they stuck out about two inches more than usual. It looked as though I had a botched Botox job. To add to the misery, burns are very painful and itch as they heal and are highly susceptible to infection.

It was October 30th, so I had my costume. The next day on the way to the hospital, I waved to the kids along the way. Some screamed in terror and some clapped for glee. All the way to the hospital, I leaned out the window waving my marigolds. The Dia de la morte' (Day of the Dead) is a religious holiday in Mexico. Mummies and marigolds are symbols for the celebration. It was good therapy for me to give those on my route a good scare from a genuine mummy traveling in their neighborhood.

I will always be grateful for the prompt, experienced, and compassionate care I received at the hospital. I kept on going daily to change dressings for about six weeks. After that, it was time to remove my eye patches permanently. My corneas had both been burned and scratched. I was lying under bright lights and trying to adjust to the light. The doctor asked, "Can you see?" I replied, "No," and I felt a surge of panic that I might be blind. My eyes finally adjusted, the shadows turned to high definition and I thanked God. My eyes had healed and were okay. I could not be in the sun and was to keep the other bandages intact for another month. My days as a mummy would end and the unveiling was successful—I was very thankful that I made a full recovery and that I would have no scarring.

The Halloween of 1980 was the most eventful I've ever had. I was probably the luckiest mummy that ever roamed the earth. I never touched or stood close to a propane tank again.

Violet

By Cathie Jacobs

S IGNS OF SPRING'S ARRIVAL WERE BREAKING THROUGH THE FROZEN crust and the dusting of the last snow was melting. Blue, white, and lavender crocuses, wild violets, and snow-on-the-mountain were the first to appear in the explosion of new beginnings. The mock cherry, lilac, and dogwood bloomed and signaled the birds to build their nests and raise their young.

One year, I decided to take the time to watch the birds in my back yard. As I sat under the pergola, perched on my favorite chair, I observed the stellar jay, very elegantly dressed in his topknot of dark blue, looking like a member of the queen's royal guard. The scrub jay next to him looked dowdy by comparison, even though his feathers were of a beautiful shade of light blue. They were obviously arguing about which of them would reside in the mock cherry tree.

The finches dive-bombed into the birdbath with a splash, showing off their chests of buttercup yellow, followed by a portly sparrow who landed in the water with a thud. A nuthatch and a chickadee waited on the lattice work for their turn to bathe. The nuthatch was a minuscule version of a stream-lined jet that flew with grace and precision, and the chickadee was a fluffy version of the nuthatch, like a Christmas-card bird. They both vied for the birdhouse hanging under the pergola for their summer home. A crow flew over, looking for nests to rob, but with no luck so far.

A red-bellied woodpecker pecked frantically at the metal on my chimney to attract a mate. It made a terrible racket, sending my Yorkie into a frenzy. I tried to scare the pesky bird off by throwing rocks at my chimney, to no avail. No mate magically appeared. He was pecking up the wrong tree. The hummingbird would appear later in spring when the firecracker fuchsia blooms, along with other bright flowers. The hummingbirds usually dart in and out of my yard, getting the nectar they deserve and then dart out with lightning speed.

I sat under the pergola watching and listening to the flutter and symphony all around the yard. Right above me, a female robin was making a nest in the wisteria atop the pergola. The wisteria would trap her. It grew so fast. I saw her abandon that site and move to the opposite side near the tree trunk. There would be no prolific growth there. A perfect spot for your home, I thought. I noticed she had a beautifully gentle demeanor. "I will name you Violet," I said out loud to myself. I surmised she was a single mother, for no male helped her build a nest, as they usually do.

Violet was very busy with trips to gather materials for her nest—strings of quackgrass, small twigs and even some mock cherry blossoms. She diligently wove all the materials into the nest, an elaborate affair indeed. She had to finish her nest soon due to her impending due date. I would note later that she finished in record time. Soon she was sitting on three perfect blue-shelled specimens. Shortly thereafter, three loud chicks with upturned beaks demanded their first meal.

The chicks soon decided they wanted out of their crowded nest and were determined to fly. And fly they did, with Violet giving encouraging chirps to fly up and down so she could lead them to safety. Mutt and Jeff landed right in front of Violet, as they were told. Merlin flew over the fence and landed in the yard next door. Violet needed him back, so she frantically tweeted at him. He returned and they all marched behind Violet for the second phase of their training, the worm-catching exercise. I had not realized that robins taught their young to eventually find their own food. She had spent a lot of time feeding them, regurgitating worms and working very hard and fast.

When I was a kid, we had an elderberry tree outside our dining room window. The robins would congregate there, imbibing the elderberries until they were drunk. Their raucous behavior caused them to run into one another. My father named one of these birds Fumblebeak, for he couldn't hang onto the berries. I guess he was pretty drunk. Probably because of this experience, my opinion of robins was not the best. I thought them irresponsible because they hung out in elderberry bushes. They were, for the most part, rather commonplace birds.

I look at robins differently now because Violet was so responsible, so sweet. She became the favorite of all my back-yard birds. She would create diversionary tactics when she taught them to dig for worms. She would hide in the ivy in one spot and leave them in another. Then she'd call them out on the grass to teach them to dig for worms. This activity would go on for several weeks.

I went out on the patio to observe Violet and her brood one morning and an eerie silence struck me. I walked over to where Violet had always been and she was not there. I looked down and noticed a trail of fluffy down and feathers. A den-izen of the night had come and snatched away the family I had such joy watching. I looked and looked, called and called, but they were not there. It was probably the predatory behavior of a cat that had silenced the happy chirps of the bird family I had loved. Every spring since then, I observe the robins that make my yard their temporary home with affection and think of Violet, building her nest and being the exceptional, caring mother she was.

SYD KANITZ'S STORY

A Northwest native, Syd Kanitz, 84, is a writer and editor with a long career as a freelance journalist and investigative reporter for Northwest newspapers and magazines, a corporate communications and public relations specialist, and columnist. She recently moved from Lake Oswego to a Tigard retirement community and continues to work part-time for the Dark Group, editing a lab pathology magazine.

Questions for My Wonderful Uncle Bill

By Syd Kanitz

O NCE YOU'VE REACHED A CERTAIN AGE, YOU CAN SPIN TALES THAT may become family legends, especially at the intersection of fact and fiction. And no one may be around to challenge them if you rewrite history. But before fact becomes fiction and fiction becomes legend, I have a lot of questions for my Uncle Bill.

I'm four years old and the year is 1937. I'm walking on a path in the woods with Mary Pemberton Byers, my mother. We are in the middle of nowhere in the Canadian Rockies. I am being told to listen for rattlesnakes and watch for them slithering out of the thick brush. So I am listening carefully, wondering what a snake must sound like, when crashing through the bushes come two handsome young men—my slow-moving Uncle Joe and my wild-eyed Uncle Bill—followed by the stern-faced Judge Pemberton.

What in the world are they doing in these faraway woods in the remote mountains of Canada while a lot of the world is on the verge of a world war? Why, fishing of course! By now, I had stared down a lot of huge dead fish bigger than I. Some of my earliest memories were of sleeping in a dark tent while these three men rose before dawn to head out to one remote lake after another.

I remember a lot of talk about possibly running into a stray bull out here in the boonies. Why were we always looking for a stray bull? In their pursuit for ever more fish-filled lakes, this group was probably cutting through one farmer's place or another.

Speaking of bulls, there is a family story that was told and retold about Uncle Bill being sent out to bring in the bull on my grandfather's farm. He was just a skinny little guy and the bull got the best of him, or so the story went. Was this just a lot of bull, Bill? Or did you really get gored?

Back in the Rockies, we're barreling down one dusty road after another, peering over the sides of steep mountains with no guardrails. We're in the judge's Model T (the Pembertons always had a car) and he's driving like a bat out of hell. Potholes are bottomless. We go down one road that is a dead end at a drop-off cliff. The entire family is packed into this car and I am standing in the back seat. Judge does a "U-ie," backing up so the rear end of the car hangs over the cliff. No one (and I will never forget this as I am standing on the seat looking out the rear window at the drop below)—no one dares to say anything to the judge as that car teeters there. He guns it, and we barely pull out. Dear Uncle Bill—was this the first time in your life you didn't say a word?

In our family, fishing is some kind of genetic addiction. The judge was an avid fisherman, as were my uncles. Bill's friend, Dr. Goodfield, in the foreword to Dr. Bill's book, *Sanity for Survival*, said Uncle Bill was the fastest man on the river he'd ever met: "He is a fisherman who fishes more like a gunfighter as he rushes a river with rod and reel, or fly-casts and spins from a boat, seldom if ever relaxing." This love of fishing has made fly-fishing addicts of my sons, who have been fishing since they could walk. I would also like to say that there are a few closet fisherwomen in the family. My sister and I both loved to fish and grew up with poles in our hands.

Back on the farm, that skinny little kid is becoming the stuff of legends again when he falls through the hole in the outhouse and it takes hours to retrieve him . . . how many times did I hear THAT story, always when family members were about to use the outhouse, of course . . . and was it true? Farm life must have been pretty rough.

I adored all my uncles but especially Uncle Bill. He was a walking show, pulling pennies from his ears, doing card tricks, throwing me into the air. About this time, a beautiful lady visited our place with my Uncle Bill. Her name was Oma. I happened to be reading the "Oz" books at the time, and it seemed to me she should be a princess called "Oma of Oz." I was in awe of her. And what do you know? They got married, more than sixty years ago. I figure that made Uncle Bill around thirty—really old for then! Where did they meet? Was it love at first sight?

For such a clean-living bunch, I remember the Pembertons always playing cards, mostly poker in big groups. Did they play for real money? Everyone sat in, including the kids. I got yelled at a lot by Uncle Bill because he didn't understand why I couldn't add numbers in my head. Still can't. He called me "precocious." I didn't know what that word meant, but it didn't sound good.

When I was a young woman and had moved to California, I had occasion to experience a wild ride with Uncle Bill through the steep streets of San Francisco. What an unforgettable experience that was! This was long before the days of Clint Eastwood and *Dirty Harry,* whom he would have put to shame.

The world's injustices (and I might add stupidities) were always of deepest concern to Uncle Bill, who made communication his lifetime work, culminating in his book, directed to world leaders—*Sanity for Survival.* Going to war in Iraq must have been a real blow, Uncle Bill. I didn't think you'd mind if I quoted in part from one e-mail: "Bin Laden calls us 'infidels'—doesn't fit; we call him 'evil'—doesn't fit. So we keep insulting until we have a war to end wars again. Anyone pushing war as a problem-solving strategy in the '90s is insane, no exceptions." He sent six letters and three e-mails to President Bush. All ignored. Did you think he would really get back to you, Uncle Bill?

There is a sequel to the "Petey the Bull" story, as told by Uncle Bill to me at his 90th birthday party. Uncle Bill had just separated Petey from the ladies of the pasture. Petey was not happy, but this had happened before. However, that day Petey was pawing the ground and snorting and Bill knew what that meant. So he said, "Petey, you're not going to act like that are you? Petey, you KNOW me and you like me, right? You wouldn't!" Whereupon Petey did. Bill recalls he ran as fast as his little legs would carry him, screaming "Maa, Maa" all the way. And that's all he remembered. He was lucky to have survived. I reckon this may have been Dr. Bill's early introduction to dealing with difficult situations (and people) and led to his sterling career as an esteemed psychiatrist who practiced in San Francisco in what was called the "Mental Block." And did you ever stop working, Uncle Bill?

Uncle Bill can't answer all the questions from his adoring niece, because he is no longer on this planet. He died at ninety-two. So I am the only one left to spin the stories and wonder which ones will finally become real legends.

ROSALYN KLIOT'S
STORIES

Rosalyn Kliot is an award-winning and published artist, with works in private and corporate collections. She is also a retired vocational rehabilitation counselor and forensic vocational expert witness at federal hearings. She is a sometimes writer, author of *My Father's Book*, a memoir, and has had her poetry and essays published in various journals and publications.

Reunion

By Rosalyn Kliot

MY 50TH HIGH SCHOOL CLASS REUNION WAS THE BEST ONE I never attended. The reunion committee had finally tracked me down and I received the invitation by email. I had missed previous reunions while either out of the country or otherwise occupied, and this time, due to back issues, I would only be able to attend this reunion vicariously via our website.

Our class of approximately five hundred was at the forefront of the "Boomers"—a generation that protested a war, marched for civil rights and women's rights, and extolled the virtues of meditation, yoga, and organic foods. We were forever known as the '60s generation, and referred to by some as self-absorbed Spock kids, who grew up privileged and entitled.

But as I read through the profiles of my classmates, I observed that we were also sons and daughters of the "Greatest Generation" and that we were those proverbial apples which had not fallen far from the tree. I was impressed with the direction that our lives had taken: physicians, lawyers, counselors, teachers, artists, writers, winners of various awards, a swami in India, a counter-culture writer/trucker/back-up musician for the Grateful Dead, an army colonel, a college professor, a rocket scientist, and many of us parents and grandparents. It was as diverse a group as one would expect from so large a class, this class of '63.

Over the years, most of my friends and I had re-located from Michigan to various parts of the country or to more exotic terrain across the seas, and we had lost contact. So I posted my photo and bio on our profile page; and just prior to and shortly after the reunion, I began hearing from classmates, some old friends, and some I had never known. Connection was re-established, oblivious to time and distance. We began filling in the blanks of our published profiles, and I realized that, over the years, we had all grown more similar than different, or at least the seeming differences of purpose and journey had become blurred and inconsequential. Many of us had reassessed our values and honed in on the privileged enclave of suburbia (despite our brief explorations of alternative lifestyles during the '60s, at least for some).

There was commonality in life's experiential education—the highs, the lows, the joys, the losses. We were life experiencers, and had seemingly developed mostly a greater vision and perhaps some wisdom that we were all in this "whatever" together, the whole and the parts matching in some sort of grandeur, with the common knowledge that we will all arrive at the same ending. Regardless of our differences, we were all connected by a more innocent and simpler time of life. I wondered at my unabashed affection for my classmates, most of whom I really had not known intimately, and shamefully, did not give much thought to for nearly half a century. If the velocity of the last fifty years is any predictor of future years (or days, weeks, months as it were), then I dare not blink. In spite of our diversity, we were now marching to a similar beat, approaching this next phase of our lives with hope, courage, and mostly the joy and wonder that we are still here.

Thanks to the extensive reach of the social network, many

of us have stayed connected by email, Facebook, etc. One has become a dear pen pal and ongoing touchstone of that earlier time. And we have maintained our reunion website in anticipation of the next reunion. Sadly, I am reminded that almost one fourth of our class did not attend the reunion because they have passed on—too soon—and so their high school graduation photos, those youthful faces so open, eager and hopeful, will forever remain etched on our profile page, looking just as they appeared back then—as part of the Niles Township graduating class of 1963.

The Other Side of Here

By Rosalyn Kliot

IT WAS ONE OF THOSE LAZY, HAZY SOUTHERN CALIFORNIA AFTER-noons in 1967, during the "Summer of Love." My kid sister, Essie, and I, along with our husbands, were picnicking at Griffith Park. We munched sandwiches while lolling in the grass and listening to "Groovin'" by the Young Rascals on the transistor radio. It was about as perfect a day as one could imagine, hazy smog notwithstanding. My then hippy spouse and I were living in Chicago while I completed my B.F.A., and he, the perpetual student, was working on his second master's degree. We were visiting my family, having camped our way cross-country. Sis and I chatted breezily as if time had not passed, and shared confidences that one can have only with a close sibling. We talked about our childhood, our folks, our spouses, our feelings, and our dreams for the future.

As children, my sister and I were inseparable, even though separated by four years. I was the elder, and followed my mom's daily mantra, "Watch your sister." I took her with me when meeting my friends at the ice-cream parlor, or attending the Saturday matinee at the Terminal movie theater (our afternoon babysitter), or strolling to and from grade school. We met at lunch time and strolled over to Mutt and Jeff's hot dog stand, where we plopped down our quarters on the counter for a Chicago Vienna hot dog, good and greasy, on a poppy seed bun, with mustard, and Chicago's unique version of relish, emerald green piccalilli.

I have a photo of us from when we were about two and six years old, and I am holding on to her hand. It reminds me of a day about that time when I held her hand while at Riverview Amusement Park. I must have let go of her hand for just an instant. It was just enough time for a stranger to stroll by and wander off with her. I watched her as they walked away, so innocent about the darker side of life. My mom, with the instincts of a momma bear for her cub, turned just in time to notice the miscreant. She dashed after him, arms flailing, shouts resonating throughout the park, until he let go of my sister's hand.

Years later, in 1974, Sis and I were driving down a highway in the San Fernando Valley to our favorite hot dog joint, Flookies, to indulge in the equivalent of the Chicago style hot dog. By that time, I was living in Orange County, in a second marriage, with a six-year-old daughter and a four-year-old stepson. Essie and I were catching up on the week's events—small talk, mostly mundane, but always worth sharing. By then, we were not just siblings, but also best friends. In the midst of our chatting, she blurted out that she had discovered a lump.

My foot slammed down on the brake, and we came to a screeching halt in the middle of the highway. Horns blasted behind me, and I could view outraged drivers through my rearview mirror. I gradually pulled over to the curb and came to a complete stop. Years later, while a practicing counselor, I would realize that I had just then entered the first stage of grief, called denial, a stage which would last for a very long time.

Sis talked about this discovery, which she had kept to herself, for months. She spoke of finally seeing a doctor, who assured her it was just a cyst. After all, she was only twenty-five, too young to be a candidate for anything serious. She had not been scheduled for a mammogram. Dumbfounded at the doctor's hasty dismissal of her symptoms, I insisted she get another opinion, which she did the following day at UCLA. Within a day, she was scheduled for a biopsy and the diagnosis was immediate.

There are some moments in our experience that defy reasonable explanation. I don't know what you call them: are they psychic, mystical, metaphysical, spiritual, wishful thinking? Or are they just confirmation that connection is inexplicable and unknown?

Some connection, however, is understandable; a mother for her child, a spouse for his or her partner, and the connection that exists between siblings. On another one of those lazy hazy Southern California afternoons, in 1978, a layer of smog blanketed Orange County like an ominous cloud. I was in a boat, drifting down a man-made lake at Knott's Berry Farm, at the very moment when my sister died. She passed over me as a whisper of absolute peace. I knew I needed to leave. When I returned home, the phone was ringing off the hook. My mother told me what I already knew. Sis had already said her good-bye.

Now, whenever I hear the song "Groovin'," I feel my sister's presence, and am reminded of a near perfect day in 1967 during the "Summer of Love."

Trekking Across
Unknown Terrain

By Rosalyn Kliot

A S A CHILD, I HAD NO SECOND THOUGHTS ABOUT RIDING MY BIKE twenty miles, or skating for hours over the frozen Chicago River, or performing back flips at will. I stood on my head without awareness of potential injury. It was a time of physical ease, without self-conscious concern for the body. Time, however, is that gracious reminder that the only constant in life is change, and that the body has a shelf life.

Over the years, I have learned not to dwell on whatever physical limitations accompany the aging process, but rather to focus on my multiple capacities. I try to follow my own counsel (that I provided my clients for more than thirty years as a counselor), which is to attend to what is positive, and not focus on whatever is perceived as negative. Yoga and swimming, walking, hiking, strength training, as well as the occasional burst of dancing with or without a partner keeps me physically fit and relatively strong, upright and footloose. Although I infrequently wax nostalgic for the days I could

carry a fifty-pound backpack on my small frame while trek-
king the mountains of the West, I now relish the ongoing
opportunity to spend time in my studio, tapping into the creative energies.

There is joy in having the time to do so and appreciation
for the frequent walks and hikes that continue to lead me
down unknown and unexplored terrain. In my imagination,
I am able to climb the Himalayas. I am grateful for whatever
physical abilities continue to bless me.

In youth we take for granted our many gifts. It has been
said so frequently that it has become one of the most overused
phrases—that youth is wasted on the young. But is that really
true? Every stage of life has its own grandeur and no years are
a waste. Youth is for youth, and, as the Byrds once reminded
us, "To every season there is a purpose."

This particular stage, which nudges us to become more
mindful of each moment, more present to each experience,
more aware of each activity, brings with it a greater appreciation of what is possible. Helen Keller wrote that "life is an
adventure or nothing at all." I might add that life is nothing
BUT an adventure, with each stage an exploration into
unknown territory. Having just reached a major milestone
birthday, and as an innately curious and optimistic human, I
am eager to explore this new terrain, in awe and wonder that I
am still here, when so many of my classmates have passed on.
I can only approach each day with gratitude and curiosity at
what is yet to come, good, bad, or otherwise. That the adventure continues is a gift, not to be taken lightly.

The proverbial mountain still calls to me. It is no longer
that physical one but the metaphorical one. There continues
to be a promise of new discoveries, new insights, and wisdom
along the way toward the apex on this remarkable journey
called life.

RONALD KUSHNER'S STORIES

Ronald Kushner was born 5 September, 1933, in London, United Kingdom. He's a Virgo. He lived with his wife, two daughters, and one son in London until 1976, where he was involved with the fashion and cosmetic industries. When he moved to the United States, he became involved in the travel industry, becoming skilled in personalized itineraries for executives in the entertainment business. He retired to Portland five years ago and wanted to write about the many chapters in his eventful life. He enjoys classes in memoir writing, guided by the two wonderful facilitators at the Lake Oswego Adult Community Center—Ronald Talney and Louise Mengelkoch.

I'm Sorry Mummy

By Ronald Kushner

THE GUILT NEVER GOES AWAY. EVEN THOUGH IT WAS ONLY A crime committed as a small boy, it has become almost impossible to forgive myself, even now after all these years.

The winter of 1947 was the coldest, harshest ever experienced by Great Britain since weather records had been kept by amateur meteorologists starting in 1659. Snow and black ice had covered everything possible in our small Victorian seaside town of Weston-super-Mare. The devastating gales that roared in over the Atlantic had pummeled the town with freezing weather for almost five months.

It had been eighteen months since peace in Europe had been declared. England had struggled valiantly for the five war years. Now, in peacetime, this nearly bankrupt small island was trying hard not to sink in a whirlpool of debt. Europe had been given vast monetary help by the United States. But England was almost totally ignored. The Labor Party politicians refused to accept that the country was absolutely broke and in very serious financial trouble. England was no longer an empire on which the sun never set.

People expected our lives to return to a state of normalcy. There would be food in the shops, you would at last be able to have new clothes, and be able to buy coal for fuel and have luxuries like hot water. We were not starving, but five years of deprivation had taken their toll on the population. The government ordered cod liver oil to be taken daily by every child; also, we had to drink the most horrible fake orange juice laced with God knows what to prevent scurvy and rickets. We were the last European country to end strict rationing of food, clothes, and furniture. If you had lost everything, furniture could only be purchased with lots of money; but more important, we still had weekly ration books.

Each person was allowed one ounce of butter, four ounces of meat (if available), one egg and one ounce of cheese. There was no coffee or tea and what happened to milk I can't remember. Our weekly two ounces of margarine substituted for cooking oil. The icing on the cake was one ounce of chocolate or sweets. New clothes were out of the question. They had only just begun to appear in stores and they always sold out in ten minutes.

There were no obese people during that time. In fact, malnutrition was the main public health problem. We received leaflets with the first banana shipment after the war, explaining how to eat the exotic fruit by peeling the skin. I wish I had kept our copy. It could be valuable now. Every woman had learned to knit. Old sweaters were unraveled, the wool reused many times to make gloves and scarves or anything that would keep you warm and help you deal with the bitter cold. If the sleeves from an old coat were worn, it didn't matter that they did not match; you sewed on the sleeves from another garment. Everyone looked like a patchwork quilt. But none of that mattered because we were still free. We had survived. Everyone anticipated the brilliant future that Prime Minister Clement Richard Attlee had promised. That was before he was elected.

The shop shelves were barren. To buy anything, you formed a queue, waited and hoped the supply would not be depleted by the time you were served. There were no private cars. You could freeze to death waiting at the bus stop. Every Monday after school, Mother would take her small woven basket and the ration books for our family of three and we would trudge through the snow and ice the two-and-a-half miles down Meadow Street to buy our food. It was vital because by Sunday evening our larder was almost totally bare.

Mother would often bake cookies on Thursday if she could see that we would have enough food to last the week. That was wonderful. But to this day, I loathe fish. Because we lived on the Atlantic coast, we had fish which was not rationed. We lived on fish. It was fish with everything. You can't make ice cream out of fish, and that is a fact of life.

We arrived at Mr. Galliard's store. Pleasantries were exchanged. He marked the ration books for that week in December and we started home through the snow and ice with our week's food in that small basket. I remember my feet and hands were frozen, even though I was wearing two pairs of gloves. They had gotten wet and the temperature was well below freezing. My feet hurt, even though father had cut out several layers of cardboard and made innersoles for my too-small shoes. There were no shoes or leather to repair shoes at that time.

I was cold but I was also hungry. Mother was always very patient but it is only now I understand the iron strength she possessed. She had known what a luxurious life could be, but never ever complained. "Ronald, we will sing loudly all the way home, then I'll put an extra blanket on the bed and we will snuggle down and keep warm," she said.

"Mother I'm cold and I'm hungry," I whined.

"I know my darling," she said. "Just take a small bite of the cheese. That will help you until we get home." I reached into the basket and searched for the three ounces of cheddar cheese that was the weekly ration for the three of us. Mother was singing loudly. I took one bite, then another, then another. Before I could stop myself, I had gorged on the whole three ounces of cheese. Suddenly it was all gone. I have tried to forget and forgive myself. But it still haunts me. I am unable to erase the vision, the sounds, or the feeling of the slightly gritty cheese taste filling my mouth.

My Unusual Wartime Education

By Ronald Kushner

Adelaide Henrietta Hodgekiss was a retired music teacher in her late 60s who had been conscripted to teach history to a class of ten-year-old boys in 1943, when I was ten years old. We thought she must be at least 150, and according to my mate, Derek Colegate, she was also a witch who could cast evil spells. I see her now as a true eccentric who has provided me with great stories at dinner parties, but at the time, I believed every horrid thing that Derek said about her.

The Christ Church Village School was built in 1863 for the young children of the small West Country seaside town of Weston-super-Mare in Somerset, England, where I grew up. Derek was our expert on the war and everything connected with Nazis due to his Germanic blonde, blue-eyed good looks and, even more important, the fact that his great-great-grandfather had been a decorated veteran on the German side during World War I. Derek was also an older guy. He wasn't just ten—he was ten years and six months. In 1943, half years were very important when you wanted to become a full member of the Christ Church Freedom Fighters Boys Gang. We learned all our history from a distant place called Hollywood; we were certainly a group of fighters to be reckoned with. Everyone had to do something to help win the war.

Derek told us in secret and on pain of death that Hodgekiss's real name was Henrietta Hitler. She was the secret wife of Adolf Hitler and had been parachuted into Weston–super–Mare by the Germans to spy on the Bristol Aircraft Factory (or BAC as we called it) where my father was engaged in secret wartime work, and her cover was being a history teacher. We thought it was our duty to king and country to protect my dad from the Nazis.

Christ Church was not geared for the influx of pupils caused by the war. Children were snatched by the government from their homes and sent to areas considered safer because of the continued bombing of London and the larger cities in the country. Many years later, it was proven that this was the most disturbing and destructive government action ever perpetuated on children of all ages, many as young as three years old.

Hodgekiss was a monochromatic woman. Her grey hair matched her grey parchment-like skin and greyish brown lips, her brownish-grey hand-knitted cardigan sweaters, her grey stockings and her black suffragette-style boots. She had clip-on glasses, what we called a Pince-nez, which helped her read fine print. We delighted in hiding them in the most obscure places we could find. "Now you dreadful, dreadful boys, where are my glasses?" she'd say in her barely audible monotone. I fell asleep in class many times. Hodgekiss learned to rule us with her cane and frequently rained a flurry of blows on boys' hands and shoulders and even, one very painful time, on my head. She knew we were horrid, dirty, nasty, filthy boys and that God would punish us for our transgressions. She also knew exactly what we all did in the boys' toilets. There is no sound like dirty young boys snickering, holding their grubby small hands over their mouths to stifle laughter. We all knew what we practiced in that hallowed place called the boys' toilet.

The school was Dickensian in every sense of the word. It was built of heavy Cornish stone bricks, the worn wood floors were splintered, the tiny, uncomfortable desks all had inkwells and were covered in ink stains and name-and-date carvings by former inmates serving out their time in their first school. The plumbing was rudimentary, and some mad Victorian architect who obviously despised and hated small boys had designed the boy's toilet.

It was built of concrete and situated far out at the end of the playground. It had no roof, so it was open to the elements. There was no washing water and I assume it got only one weekly cleaning by the school caretakers. I'm sure there was a shortage of carbolic for cleaning due to the war. The trough ran about six feet long and there were only three "big job" stalls made private by wooden half-doors painted a diuretic shade of green. Suspended over the broken wooden toilet seats were three iron water closets, one with no pull-chain, just a piece of string. They regularly froze over solid in the winter, which was a major issue. We would burst rather than defecate in the winter.

Needless to say, the smell of urine was constant. I have encountered such toilets as an adult travelling in third-world countries. But to us boys it was almost like paradise. It was a respite from the drudgery of learning. We always had a great time in the lavatory. It was like fighting the war in the urinal trenches. It was competition time as we lined up to see who could project their pee right over the wall into the school playground. Obviously, the bigger boys had an advantage. Derek Colgate was often the champion. If you could wet some passing girl, you were king for a day. We knew Hodgekiss knew. We knew the headmaster knew. We all knew, but it was source of pleasure and delight to us.

Hodgekiss single-handedly killed history for me. I did not

understand that history could be a wonderful subject until I was in college. You see, Hodgekiss taught us only one thing—how to brew mead. We learned nothing about the Tudors, the Stuarts, the Anglo-Saxons, the Romans, the Georgians or Edwardians—just the making of an alcoholic beverage, which in Roman times had been called Sima. All that honey, fruit, yeast, and fermentation. She assured us that mead had been a favorite drink of Henry VIII. This knowledge of her family recipe, she assured us, would prove to be one of the most valuable skills required for our adult lives.

Each term, she trundled in a large wooden wheelbarrow, small oak fermenting barrels, honey, yeast and any fruit that was available, which, because of the war, was very little. A note was passed in class that Hodgekiss had been breeding killer bees, not just for the honey but because she was Adolf's wife, and they were going to be let loose and sting everyone to death. It was another fiendish Nazi secret weapon.

Some days we actually had two history periods—one before lunch and one after lunch. All the male teachers had been drafted into the armed forces and only the very, very old male teachers escaped conscription. They were, without exception, dreadful, and most of them hated young children. But you worked where the government assigned you. We also had a few elderly dinner ladies. I am unable to call them cooks. I am sure that they did their very best to feed us, but there was a scarcity of food during the height of the war.

We ate off tin plates, and drank from chipped mugs. Mother did her very best to send me to school with something that I could eat, but we did not know or understand that we were constantly hungry. We lived for Mother's American relatives to send us food parcels through The Red Cross containing items like candy and tins of exotic things like Pillsbury dough, enabling mother to make cookies. Everything packed in those wonderful magic parcels, all of which were unobtainable in a small Somerset town at the height of the war, was truly magnificent. I heard the word utopia used to describe the United States of America. I had to go to the dictionary to understand the meaning of the word. Our gang traded food items with each other. It was like we had our own little black market. I learned at a very early age that this land called America was a land of food, movies, comics, and finally, that wonder, Hershey chocolate bars.

We had fish constantly because we lived on the Atlantic Coast so it wasn't rationed. I vowed on VE Day I would never ever in my whole life let one bite of any fish pass my lips. Many years later, I was able to enjoy fish once again. School dinners also killed custard for me. Decades later, my wife made trifle and custard cream prepared with the best ingredients and laced with dollops of good old Harvey's Bristol sherry. It seems you can change your eating habits after all when you're grown up. And now I am very grown-up indeed.

I don't know whatever became of Hodgekiss, but Derek became a scientist dealing with nuclear fusion. He lived in Ireland for several years, and eventually went to work for the U.S. Defense Department in Washington, D.C. Maybe he did know something we didn't.

DIANE LUND-MUZIKANT'S STORIES

Diane Lund-Muzikant, who grew up in North Minneapolis, is a retired investigative journalist who earned a reputation as a champion for unbiased and uncensored reporting of Oregon's health care industry. She's also proud to be a twenty-three-year breast cancer survivor and an adventure traveler, having reached Mt. Everest Base Camp despite being kicked off the group trek by the leader who insisted she wasn't strong enough to make the 17,598 ft. climb.

The Recital

By Diane Lund-Muzikant

MOTHER WAS ABOUT TO IRON MY YELLOW TAFFETA DRESS WHEN the doorbell rang. It wasn't often I had new clothes. Money was tight. It was June 1944. World War II was raging. We relied on ration stamps for food and for kerosene.

That didn't stop my dad from hitting up the liquor store. I often wondered where he found the money to buy caseloads of Pabst Blue Ribbon since he gave his paycheck to mother every Friday.

Mother had taken me to a clothing store on Plymouth Avenue, a few blocks from where we lived. The moment I tried on the taffeta dress I fell in love with it. The dress was sparkling white, with tiny red buttons on the back, and a red sash around the waist. Underneath was a crinoline petticoat made of horsehair and cotton.

There was even a matching bonnet with a red ribbon that tied under my chin. I buckled the straps on the patent leather Mary Jane shoes, and twirled around the store on my tippy-toes, pretending to be a ballerina.

Grandma Esther had come over to help mother make a

lemon sponge cake for the party after my recital. She saw my dress on the ironing board. "Diane, you're going to be the most beautiful girl on stage tomorrow afternoon," she said.

When she leaned over to kiss my cheek, I noticed a small package in her hands. I ripped off the gilded wrapping paper and gold ribbon. Inside was a charm bracelet. Tiny ballet figurines dressed in pink tutus with bows in their hair hung from the silver chain. Grandma clasped the bracelet around my left wrist. "My mother gave this to me when I was six years old, the same age you are. Now it's yours forever." Her soft voice made me blush.

Then Grandma scooted into the kitchen. A few minutes later I heard her arguing with Mother about whether the egg yolks needed to be separated from the egg whites before stirring them into the sugary batter. Mother didn't have a clue about how to make a cake or, for that matter, anything else about cooking. But she wasn't about to let Grandma tell her what to do.

That's when I noticed the iron plugged into the wall socket. Mother's so busy. I'll iron those wrinkles from my dress myself, I thought.

The iron had tiny holes on the bottom where the steam shot out. I grabbed onto the handle with my left arm but couldn't lift it. So I changed hands. The iron glided over my dress—the puffy sleeves, the Peter Pan collar, the long flowing skirt.

This was the first time I used an iron. Mother had always forbidden me, saying I'd burn myself. Well I'm showing her. She'll be so proud of me. But no matter how many times I tried, the wrinkles wouldn't come out. I remember watching mother wet her fingers with a few drops of water, then touch the bottom of the iron to see if it was hot. So I did the same thing. But when I lifted the iron again, it slipped out of my hand and landed on my left forearm, a few inches from my new bracelet.

My arm turned bright red. A blister started forming. "Someone help me. I burned my arm. It's on fire!"

Grandma ran into the room. "Oh my gracious. What have you done to yourself? We need to get you to a doctor right away."

My screams woke up Uncle Neil, who'd driven Grandma to our house. He grabbed his keys and began carrying me to his car.

"Put her down," said Mother. "I can take care of my daughter. I don't need your help." Mother led me to the kitchen sink and plunged my arm into cold running water. Then she dabbed some white cream on my arm from the medicine cabinet, wrapped a gauze bandage around the burn, and fastened it with adhesive tape. "The skin didn't break," she said. "You'll be just fine." Tears trickled down my face. I wanted mother to comfort me, to tell me that my arm was going to be okay. "Enough drama out of you, Diane," she said. "Now get to bed before you have another accident."

"But what about my new dress? Did it get ruined?"

"Fortunately not. But you're never to use an iron again. Do you understand?"

Grandma started walking toward me, her arms open wide. Mother shooed her out, slamming the front door so loud it sounded like a bolt of thunder.

I crept into the bedroom, and climbed to the top bunk. Alan, my older brother, fiddled with his new transistor radio. "Looks like you messed up again, little Sis."

In the next room, I heard mother talking on the phone. "Bernie, you'll never believe what your clumsy daughter did to herself tonight."

That night, I dreamed that I lived in Grandma's house near North Commons park. She pushed me high in the air on the swings and caught my feet when I slid down the curvy slide. In the dream, I didn't have to share a bedroom with Alan, who made fun of my big ears, saying I looked like an elephant. I soaked in Grandma's claw-foot bathtub until all the bubbles disappeared. When I dripped water on the floor or clogged the toilet with too much paper, she didn't raise her voice or use foul words. We huddled under the electric blankets at night,

Grandma telling me funny stories about monkeys who ran off with bananas after escaping from the zoo. Then she'd kiss me goodnight. Grandma always cooked whatever I wanted for breakfast—strawberry pancakes or waffles, oatmeal sprinkled with raisins and brown sugar and, my favorite, apple strudel. And she kept a bottle of chocolate milk in her icebox.

I always thought my Grandma was special. But I lived with her only in my dreams.

MY RECITAL DAY

The next morning, I woke up in a panic. I tried to calm my nerves by going back to sleep. Mother peeked into the bedroom.

"Get out of bed right now, Diane. Otherwise we're going to be late."

I didn't budge.

Alan yanked off my bed covers and pulled the pillow from under my head.

"Ha, ha, got you now." He ran out of the bedroom, grinning from ear to ear.

My taffeta dress hung in the closet but I couldn't find the crinoline petticoat.

Mother had toasted a few slices of Wonder Bread, slathering them with margarine and strawberry jam.

"My petticoat's missing. Have you seen it?" Alan sat in the kitchen, a smirk on his face. He yanked the petticoat from under his chair. It landed by my feet.

"Stop fussing around you two," said Mother. "Let's get out of here."

The sun peeked out from the clouds as we boarded the streetcar. I squeezed by a grey-haired lady who poked her parasol in my ribs. Alan found an empty seat near a window. I clutched the hand rail. I wanted Mother to tell him to get up so I could sit down.

She didn't seem to notice. She only said, "You better not mess up today after all the time and money I've spent on those lessons."

Alan began poking his fingers in his ears and wiggling his hands. "Na, Na, Na. I bet you'll forget every word when you go on stage."

Dad was waiting in front of the McPhail School of Music. He worked the graveyard shift at the Hiawatha Railroad station, cleaning the train's carriages. He'd mop the floors, haul away the cigar butts and unclog the toilets. Sometimes he'd bring home Hershey candy bars and packets of Juicy Fruit gum left on the trains. Once he found a five-dollar bill lying on a seat cushion. That night our family went out for Chinese food.

I could hardly wait to show him the charm bracelet Grandma had given me. Before I could say anything, he shook his fist in my face.

"Why were you so clumsy last night? Look at your arm all bandaged up."

"Bernie, leave Diane alone. Don't you realize she has a recital today?"

Mother led us down the street to Furman Drugs, a few blocks away. Inside, a white-jacketed soda jerk stood in front of the marble countertop. I clambered up on a bar stool and swiveled around. Mother ordered a cherry phosphate for me, a chocolate one for Alan. We often stopped here after my lessons on Saturday afternoons. Once mother took me to the Orpheum Theater to see Judy Garland in *Meet me in St. Louis*. I sang "The Trolley Song" all the way home.

When we got back to McPhail, Dad was talking to Mrs. Hutchinson, my elocution teacher. She held out her hands to greet my mother. I snuck behind so she wouldn't notice my bandaged arm. "Milly, you can be so proud of your daughter," she said.

Mother patted me on the head and led us to the front row. She saved a seat for Grandma. One by one, young musicians appeared on stage—a clarinetist, a drummer, a cello player, a violinist, a flute player. The audience clapped boisterously after each performance.

Then Mrs. Hutchinson called my name. As I climbed the wooden steps to the stage, the gauze bandage wrapped around my arm started to unravel. It was too late to turn around.

"Diane, what have you done to yourself?" She looked at my blistered arm. By now, the bandage lay sprawled on the stage.

I didn't know what to say. If I told the truth, that I'd burned myself because the iron slipped out of my hands, she'd wonder why my mother would have let her six-year-old daughter use an iron.

If I made up a story about getting too close to a hot frying pan sizzling with grease, my mother would scold me for telling a lie.

So I said nothing.

The silence seemed endless. My hands started to quiver, my knees buckled.

Closing my eyes for a few seconds, I took a deep breath. Then I remembered what Mrs. Hutchinson had taught me. Enunciate each word clearly. Don't talk too fast, speak loudly so everybody can hear you and smile.

Just then Grandma rushed down the aisle, the veil on her black pompadour hat resting on her forehead. Waving her arms in the air, she blew me a kiss.

I began to recite the poem I practiced in class—"Peach Pie." The words spilled out of my mouth so clearly, I almost forgot I was standing in front of an audience. I bowed to the sound of applause. Grandma hugged me. Alan gave me a high five. Mother handed me a red rose bud. I was so choked up I could barely speak. When I looked at Dad, he shifted his eyes away from me and I started crying. Grandma wiped my tears away with her handkerchief, sneering at Dad.

My elocution lessons had started that summer when Mother decided I needed to overcome my shyness. I didn't have any friends. I would sit in my bedroom alone, playing with dolls, and not talk. At Grant Elementary School in north

Minneapolis where I'd just completed first grade, I sat in the back row, never raising my hand when Mrs. Bryce, my teacher asked a question.

Once when she called on me. I shook my head rather than say anything, even though I knew the answer.

Mother cashed in a war bond that Grandma had given her to pay for the classes. Dad didn't find out about the classes until Alan snitched on her.

"Why does Diane need to learn how to talk? She just needs to open her mouth," he said. Mother didn't respond when Dad spouted off.

The first day I met Mrs. Hutchinson, she looked different than anyone else I'd seen before. She had the brightest blue eyes, and wore a pearl choker around her neck. Her shirtwaist dress had wide buttons all the way down the skirt. The black seams on her nylons were perfectly straight.

Every Saturday, I'd recite a poem or story from memory. If I had trouble pronouncing a word, Mrs. Hutchinson whispered it in my ear. She only reprimanded me if I laughed when someone slurred a word. "I'm here to help you gain confidence so you won't be shy," she said.

After my recital, the elocution lessons ended. I didn't see Mrs. Hutchinson again, but she taught me a valuable lesson—to believe in myself.

The Phone Call That Changed My Life

By Diane Lund-Muzikant

I RECOGNIZED HER CALM VOICE RIGHT AWAY. SHE WAS CALLING TO share the test results. Why was she telling me this over the phone? Shouldn't I be coming into her office to hear the news? Didn't she realize I was home alone, that my husband was still at work?

After she hung up, I sat motionless in front of the computer screen, whimpering. "How could this be happening to me? What had I done wrong?" I thought about calling Michael at the pharmacy but hesitated, unsure how he'd react. Fear crippled me.

It had been another dreary day in Portland—the skies a solemn grey. But the weather seldom impacted my mood. I'd never felt so content. A newlywed. I spent every night embracing Michael, showering him with kisses before we fell asleep in each other's arms. I was proud of my daughter, who'd been accepted into a Ph.D. program at Wayne State University to become a clinical psychologist. And I was the editor of a successful newsletter that investigated Oregon's health care industry.

The phone rang again. I hesitated. Perhaps she was calling back to say there had been a mistake. My hands trembled as I slowly lifted the receiver to my ear.

A man's voice said I'd won a free all-expense trip to Las Vegas. All I needed to do was take a tour of the Desert Paradise Resort, a time-share condominium. I slammed down the phone, biting back tears.

An hour later, Michael came home, a haggard look on his face. He'd been filling prescriptions all day without taking a lunch break after the other pharmacist had called in sick. Michael could see something was troubling me. My eyes were puffy and reddish, my face pale, my hands twitched.

He asked if I had finished the story about a prominent doctor being dismissed by Legacy Health for indiscretion. I shook my head no. I'd been too busy with a more important project. We sat down to dinner. Michael ate ravenously, pulling the chicken off the bones, sipping a glass of red wine. I fiddled with my fork, but couldn't eat a thing.

My voice trembled as the words flowed out of my mouth. The biopsy results had come back. I had breast cancer. The surgeon hadn't seen anything alarming when she examined my breast, even though calcifications, small calcium deposits, had shown up on the mammogram. Usually they were benign. Not this time.

Michael held me in his arms, repeating over and over again that he'd stay by my side forever, no matter the outcome.

"I'll do anything I can to comfort you. We can fight this together, Diane. You're not alone. I love you dearly. You're a strong woman. This isn't a death sentence."

Every Friday night we lit the Shabbat candles, repeating the Hebrew blessing. That night was no exception. When I lifted my hands to bring in the light and closed my eyes, I remembered the first time I saw Michael at a barbecue for

Jewish singles. He'd been separated from his wife; I'd been single for eighteen years.

He seemed so gentle, so kind, so willing to please me, unlike Charlie, who always seemed wrapped up in his own problems.

A year earlier, Charlie had asked me to marry him, proposing on Christmas Day, a solitaire diamond ring in his hand. As I contemplated saying yes, the phone rang. My mother, who had been struggling with pneumonia after being diagnosed with lung cancer, had died. I needed to fly to Minneapolis right away to make funeral plans and console my father.

Charlie promised he'd wait. But when I returned home, I found him in bed with the cleaning lady. I often wonder if he could have tolerated my angry outbursts upon learning I had cancer. After Michael and I met, I began noticing splotches of blood in my underpants. I couldn't be going through menopause. That had happened ten years ago.

The ultrasound was inconclusive, the images too blurry. The doctor couldn't tell if the polyps were malignant. She recommended a hysterectomy. I worried about losing Michael. We'd only known each other nine months.

The sun just peeked out from the clouds when the biopsy results came back. I was cancer free. Michael acted so giddy he nearly tipped over my cup of cappuccino as he threw his arms around me. Then he ran down to the hospital lobby bringing back a helium balloon emblazoned with the words, "I failed cancer."

Two years later Michael and I were married. An artist, the wife of a rabbi from Eugene, designed our Ketubah, our marriage contract. During the ceremony, we took turns reciting the words I'd written professing our love for each other. "Each day I spend with you is a gift from God. I promise to stay by your side forever, listen to you without being judgmental and support you during times of turmoil. May God enrich us with peace and joy; may laughter lighten our lives."

Why hadn't I included the words "good health?" By now it

was too late. Cancer had already invaded my life. On January 26th, the surgeon removed my left breast. I woke feeling disoriented. A part of me was gone, the breast where I had fed my infant daughter. I was terrified. I shrieked but no one heard my voice. I kept ringing the buzzer. The nurses were busy. No one came. Michael was at work. I closed my eyes. Perhaps I was having a dream? No, a nightmare.

Early the next morning, Rabbi Gary, who had married us, showed up unexpectedly at the hospital. He stood at the stood at the edge of my bed, saying a healing prayer when the surgeon walked in. Another test result. She had removed sixteen lymph nodes from under my left arm to determine if the cancer had spread. One was positive. I needed to make an appointment with the oncologist.

I was desperate to rid myself of any lingering cancer cells that, I was told, could lay dormant inside my body for years. A clinical trial seemed the best opportunity. I was chosen for two rounds of Adriamycin, one of the most powerful and strongest cancer drugs, every three weeks, and one round of Cytaxin.

I sat in the soft leather chairs in Dr. Seligman's office, a blanket wrapped around my lap, as the poisons flowed through my port, attacking the cancer cells. I lost my appetite. The only foods that appealed to me were grilled cheese sandwiches and sugar wafer cookies. The taste of coffee disgusted me and still does to this day. Michael encouraged me to try Pho, the Vietnamese soup. I downed the slippery noodles so fast he thought I might gag.

I found clumps of hair on my pillowcase when I woke up, and had my head shaved and bought a wig. When my hair started growing back, I dyed it bright orange and green, covering my head with a baseball cap. I was almost turned away at a fancy restaurant. Hats weren't allowed, the concierge told me. When I lifted my cap, he dropped his chin and led us to a table.

Within a month, my red blood count plunged. I became

anemic. The oncologist ordered a blood transfusion. Michael held my hand as I lay on the hospital gurney waiting for the blood to flow through my veins.

Looking down, he noticed something shiny on the bottom hospital rail. It was a Jewish Star of David. Nobody in the hospital seemed to know where it had come from. I cupped the charm in my hands, not letting go until I fell asleep. From that day forward I began calling myself a cancer survivor.

MARIA McCARTHY'S
STORIES

Maria Moldovan McCarthy was born in Tarneveni, Romania. She immigrated to America after World War II. She earned a B.S degree in education and a master's in art education from Ball State University, in Muncie, Indiana. She is a retired high school art teacher and a mother, grandmother, wife, sister, and friend.

Our Farewell Christmas

By Maria McCarthy

IT WAS A DAY SHORTLY BEFORE CHRISTMAS IN 1945. MY MOTHER sat with her mother and sister in the kitchen/great room of her family home in Panade, the Romanian village where she'd grown up. All sorts of activities took place in that room—cooking, storytelling, great meals, simple meals and best of all, lots of family fun. The three women must have been very sad. It was the last Christmas they would ever spend together as a family. In spite of that, their determination to carry on the same holiday traditions with as much love and joy as possible was admirable and remarkable.

We children were sitting on the floor playing with our toys and not aware of what the women were discussing or what tasks they were involved with. I remember gold and silver paint on the table. However, I did not connect their activity with anything in particular. We would soon make the trip to our grandparents' village for our annual Christmas celebration.

Christmas was mostly about tradition. The holiday was filled with stories, music and, of course, an abundance of amazing food. On Christmas Eve day we polished those ugly brown high-top shoes we all wore. That evening, the shoes were placed outside the door, awaiting a visit from *Mos Craciun* (pronounced "Mosh Crashoon"). The legend is that *Mos Craciun* ("Old Father Christmas or Saint *Niculaie*") traveled from house to house filling those little shoes with walnuts painted gold and silver (hence the gold and silver paint that the ladies were using), hard candies, fruit, nuts, and small presents, usually a toy.

Maria carried on those traditions in America. How happy were we that *Mos Craciun* found us! On Christmas morning we shrieked with delight as we threw open the door in anticipation of our clean, polished little shoes full of Christmas treats. Naturally we were told that only "good" little children found their shoes full of treats. If you were naughty—well—you had shoes filled with COAL. (I think the same legend is told in many countries!)

Certainly all children in the village found their shoes full of treats. We were so happy to discover our pretty silver and gold walnuts, candy, toys, and the coveted tangerines, dates, and oranges. The last three items were imported from Turkey. Those unattractive brown leather high-tops never looked so beautiful!! Can you imagine if we filled our children's little Nikes with such simple delicacies? I am grateful that I still remember the joy the three of us felt, not to mention the happiness of our parents, grandparents, aunts and uncles as they watched our discovery.

It was a happy and memorable last Christmas. We attended the village church, sang Christmas carols (called *colinde*) while our family expressed such joy, in spite of the knowledge that in a few short weeks we were sailing to a new home in America.

After the service, we retreated to the family home for an abundant holiday feast that had required days and days of preparation. My grandfather butchered one of his fine hogs and made all sorts of sausages, including bacon and smoked meats in his smoke house. We had *sarmale* (stuffed cabbage rolls), *mamaliga* (polenta) and roast pork. After the main meal, we had unbelievable pastries like *cornulete* (butter croissants filled with ground walnuts, sugar, and honey). For days, the women had baked an assortment of breads called *cozonati* (pronounced "cozonach"). Some were filled with nuts and golden raisins, and, my favorite, ground poppy seeds mixed with sugar and brandy. They were all so tasty because they'd been prepared with love.

Once settled in our new country, those European traditions continued. For a couple of years, *Mos Craciun* (now Santa Claus) even remembered to fill our little shoes with goodies. My parents continued many of the traditions for the remainder of their lives. I miss those wonderful holidays with all the food, song and laughter. I can still remember my father coming home with a butchered, dressed hog the week before Christmas. Like my grandfather, he made all sorts of sausages and delicacies from that hog. Our mother prepared a variety of baked goods, prepared with such skill and dedication. Her baking created aromas that never faded from our memories. Try as I may, I just can't duplicate her wonderful baking but I'm still trying!

Holidays are still fun, but different. While I love and enjoy my family, it seems to be missing that "special something." Is it that life was so simple then and we took the time to savor and embrace it? Do we expect too much today? Have we forgotten how to slow down and enjoy what we are so lucky to have? As for me, I miss those days. I cherish the memories and I look at the present in a different light. No, they're not the same kind of memories but still good ones. I look at all the friends and family we are so fortunate to have. We had only each other growing up. Our relatives lived in a country too far to travel to for holidays. Mostly, I am thankful that I can still recall so vividly that last family Christmas.

The Journey

By Maria McCarthy

The time had come for the five passengers to disembark. They
would share excitement, joy, and an overwhelming sadness as
they left the sailors on the SS Benjamin Rush, the navy ship
that carried them to America—a month-long voyage leaving
them with so many new memories and new experiences.

It was aboard this ship that they learned their first English
words and phrases, many they didn't understand, others that
they would say and use the rest of their lives. It was on the ship
that they saw and met their first black man. He was the cook.
At every meal, Cook would go to each person seated at long
tables, walking quickly, pointing his forefinger to each and in
a sing-song manner ask, "You coffee, you coffee, you coffee?"
Not knowing what that meant but liking the sound of it, we
would chime in with him, which caused laughter from the
sailors in the dining hall. Cook not only introduced us to new
words and phrases, but to our favorite treat on board—saltine

crackers with a mound of orange marmalade on top—to this day, still a favorite.

Being on board a big navy ship was exciting. However, the sailors had work to do and we were bored at times. Mother Maria experienced a lot of sea sickness, leaving Father Peter in charge of the three kids. When time was available, the sailors would play games with us. They even built a swing that took us high in the air, complete with frightful screams and lots of laughter. Happy memories had come to an end but not forgotten over these many years.

We packed up in anticipation of our journey's end. We each had a small suitcase holding our few items. Mine included my favorite dress—powder blue with pink rose buds—a sweater, a couple changes of clothes, socks and my doll. The boys had their clothes, and, of course, we all wore the same kind of shoes—brown leather high-tops with laces. Even at four, I had a strong dislike for them. Peter and Maria had few possessions. The plan was that once we were settled, they would buy things in America. My mother sold her gold wedding ring before leaving Romania, providing a little more money for our life in the new country. Leaving the ship and heading for shore was tearful as well as exciting. We had no idea what to expect.

Strangers were waiting to greet us when we disembarked. But they spoke Romanian and English. It was so good to understand every word spoken. They hugged and kissed us as if we were their long-lost family returning to them after a long absence. They gave us our first American gifts—a doll for me, and for each of the boys, big powder-blue, metal pistols—not cowboy guns but pistols! Then they proceeded to teach us a new string of English words. "Stick em up, gimme your money!" Naturally, we had no idea what this meant, but curiously watched as all the host adults raised their hands in the air. Welcome to America! Honestly, these were really nice people. Later, those blue pistols would take on personalities of their own, but that's another story. Once we were alone, our parents assured us this was not a phrase we would ever be using and explained why.

Our hosts were ready to take us to their home. We were tired and hungry and looking forward to stable ground. The Baltimore family had their own car. We were in awe. Cars were pretty big in those days, so It didn't seem at all crowded with four adults and three children. We were on our way to another new adventure.

We were guests in their home for nearly a week, taking care of immigration stuff and planning the trip to our new and (what we thought was) our final destination. Peter and son George were American citizens. Maria and the other two children were not. They had entered the country with visitor visas and the plan was to become naturalized citizens in the near future. Prior to the war, any child born to an American citizen on foreign land was automatically a citizen. If an American citizen married a person from a different country, they too would become American. I believe there may have been an abundance of marriages and births on foreign lands, thus causing a huge influx of immigrants during the war. A suspension of that existing law was enforced until after the war, so we were a half-and-half family—half American, half Romanian. We remained so for several years.

Our Flat at 513-1/2 Court Street

By Maria McCarthy

S ATURDAY NIGHT, *BATH NIGHT IN THE KITCHEN.* MARIA WAS BUSY boiling water in every available pot . . . not that we had many. It was a cold water flat (no running hot water) so water had to be boiled for washing dishes, laundry, and for weekly baths. The gas cooking stove was ablaze with boiling water that turned the kitchen into a steamy sauna.

We had a bathroom but it only contained a toilet—no sink, no bathtub. None of the flats had sinks and tubs. The kitchen sink was the only sink. For baths we had a large zinc tub. It was large enough for an adult or two small children. I was always first to bathe, the boys followed. Maria made her own soap—no fragrance—but not bad. The baths were quick so the water would stay warm enough for the duration of the baths. There were lots of giggles and laughter, shrieks too when soap got in our eyes. Ouch! Peter and Maria took baths after the children were off to bed.

Many Romanian families had pet names for their children.

We had ours. George was Gita (Gitza), Emil was Milu (Meelu), and I was Pica (Peeka). It meant "little." We were called these names all during our early years. The boys graduated to their given names while I was called Marioara (muddywara) for most of my life . . . but only by my parents.

We loved our cold water flat—it was the best. Our building was made of red bricks. It had two levels—four flats on the bottom and four on top. The front of the building had two entrances, one at each end with a wooden stairway and a door to the first-floor flats in each entrance. The stairs led to the upstairs flats. The stairways were dark and kind of scary with poor lighting.

Our first flat was at one end on the second level. After two years, we moved to the other end of our building, on the same level. Our second flat had a better toilet and was in overall better condition. I really didn't understand what that meant exactly at the time. It looked almost identical to the one we had moved from. All flats had the same floor design. Three rooms—a front room, a middle room and of course a kitchen.

Each complex had three identical buildings. From the back of our building, we could see a building across from us and one to the right of us. Each building had a porch that ran across the length of the structure. A stairway off the center of the porch led to a courtyard surrounded by sheds, one for each tenant. The sheds were used for storage of coal which provided fuel for the kitchen stoves.

There were two structures made of cement blocks in the center of the courtyard. Three walls were about four feet high. The front was open and there was no roof. They were our garbage containers. We had no bags, only pails. Needless to say, the stench in the summer was dreadful, not to mention the rats and other vermin they attracted. Children were not permitted to play in the courtyard for obvious reasons. Garbage was collected once a week. Thank God for parks and playgrounds! Can you imagine carrying buckets of coal up those stairs and buckets of garbage down to the pits???

The porches and spaces underneath were used for drying laundry and for potted plants. When it was not too stinky, tenants would socialize in the back of their homes. We could see the back doors of the neighbors across from us and to the side of us. It was not long before we all knew each other. Memories of these families are still vivid. There was a family of four from Hungary. The children, Steven and his sister Anuka, were a couple years older than the three of us. Steven played the violin. Boy, could he create beautiful music. He played with their door open and his music could be heard throughout the courtyard.

I loved sitting on the stairs listening to that beautiful music. Steven practiced all the time, and I bet his parents never had to nag him to do so. To this day, the violin is my favorite instrument. I don't play it, but I just love the sound of the beautiful music it creates, some happy and some so emotional that it brings tears to my eyes. Years later Steven and I ended up teaching in the same high school.

Anuka was also musical, although I can't recall her instrument. She was a beautiful blonde young lady with an angelic look, and had small gold hoops in her pierced ears. As for me, I still wore my ugly brown leather high-top laced shoes.

Next door to the Hungarians lived Mamie, her policeman husband Joe, and her elderly father. Mamie and Joe did not have children, so they sort of adopted me, taking me to downtown Indianapolis for movies and sometimes dinner or ice cream. Mamie and Joe were the first people we knew with a television.

Televisions were brand new, with only a few programs each night. My favorite was *Kukla, Fran and Ollie*. Some of you may remember them. Mamie and Joe had their very own telephone too. It would be several years before we had a TV or a telephone.

In the building to the side of us we made two friends, Jimmy and Joyce. Jimmy was Emil's age, while Joyce and I were the same age. Shortly after we became friends, my parents did not permit us to go to their flat. Soon it became obvious that the father had a serious drinking problem. The neighbors heard the loud violent arguments coming from their apartment. After each fight, their mom would appear with cuts, bruises and sometimes black eyes. One time, the argument was so violent that the father broke her jaw. It had to be wired shut, allowing her only a liquid diet. It was hard to believe that someone could do that sort of damage to a family. I don't believe the children were abused physically, but certainly they must have had some emotional scars.

These were just a few of the neighbors and friends we had while we lived at 513-½ Court Street. We made many friends during the five years that we lived there. Some remained life-long friends with our parents.

GLENNIS CEDARHOLM
McNEAL'S STORIES

Glennis Cederholm McNeal, 80, is a retired journalist, public relations practitioner and freelance writer who has lived in Oregon since 1959. She is writing about growing up in the Western States of Montana, Wyoming, Utah, South Dakota, and Oregon.

Western States of Mind: When Mineral Water Fails

By Glennis Cedarholm McNeal

"TICK SHOTS TODAY." THE ALARMING WORDS SHOT FROM STU-
dent to student in our small school in Thermopolis,
Wyoming. The message was as urgent as an announcement
that snakes were loose in the hallways. Classrooms emptied
of students as we lined up in the gymnasium. My stomach
knotted in dread.

I knew that at Brownie Scout Camp, the mothers in charge
made us stand naked in the dark while they searched our hair-
less bodies by flashlight. I didn't realize they were looking
for ticks. I didn't know that Rocky Mountain spotted fever,
caused by a tick bite, could affect the skin, brain, heart, and
even the kidneys. Scientists died of what we called "tick fever"
while researching a vaccine.

I did know, and believed with all my heart, that nothing
could be worse than these preventive shots. Scared and trem-
bling, I inched forward in the line. Nurses sat at card tables.
One of these agents of pain armed with syringe, rubbing

alcohol, cotton pads, and bandages, beckoned me. Her white uniform and starched cap made her monstrous. The room reeked of nervous sweat and pungent antiseptics.

"These shots don't hurt," she said crossly when I winced and shrank away from her. Easy for her to say, I thought. She wasn't being swabbed, stabbed and swabbed again. She finished by slapping an adhesive bandage on my arm. Around me, some students, like my younger brother Billy, cried. Older boys swaggered out of the gym to show how tough they were.

The nurse was correct to say the shot didn't hurt. She should have added, "Today." For the next few days the injection site was painful, particularly when boys punched you on the bandage. Smart kids moved it to their other arm. In 1948, when I was eleven, smallpox and tick vaccines were the only immunizations we knew. A circular scar on my thigh proved I was vaccinated against smallpox. I was immune to measles, mumps, rubella, and chickenpox because I'd already had them and recovered. Tick shots, on the other hand, were an annual spring ordeal.

Thermopolis, population 3,500, had been a health care Mecca ever since 1896, when Chief Washakie deeded local thermal hot springs to the white man. Residents believed the sulfurous mineral water could cure anything. Drink it, bathe in it, believe in it. It was good stuff. Physicians were needed despite the healing waters. Dr. Nels Vicklund and Dr. Benjamin Gitlitz treated patients, mostly on an emergency basis. Well-child checkups? No such thing. If you were well, you didn't need a doctor.

Patients believed their own doctor was a medical genius and the other doctor was dangerously incompetent. "I heard that Dr. Gitlitz walked out of the newborn nursery and left the door open," huffed a fellow student. "Those babies could have caught hospital germs." She learned of this alarming incident from the hospital cleaning lady.

An angry neighbor said, "My cousin went to Vicklund with a bad pain in his side. Vicklund told him to go home and take mineral oil and come back the next day for a full exam. Well! The mineral oil made him move his bowels and the pain went away." Outrage radiated from her every pore. "Imagine scaring someone into thinking he needed an exam when all he really needed was an enema."

Alternative health care providers pitched in. The Assembly of God church laid hands on people who needed healing. We watched the congregation through its open door and heard them speak in tongues. The ramshackle building bore the words ASS. OF GOD. It was written with a wide brush dipped into cheap black paint. The paint dripped before it dried. The final letter looked like an "O." "Ass of Goo" became the non-believer's code word for "faith healing."

A traveling optician came to town several times a year to give eye exams. If you needed vision correction, you waited anxiously for eyeglasses to come in the mail weeks later. Dental work was available in Worland, a town thirty miles north. Orthodontia meant a drive to Casper, 130 miles south and east.

It seems to me now that each health care option could be described in just three words. Health care? **Suck it up**. You saw a doctor if you were seriously ill, and sometimes, not even then.

Dental care? **Yank it out**. It made no sense to spend time and money on fillings when dentures solved the problem.

Mental health? **Get over it.** A quiet playmate from our neighborhood knew all about that remedy. He told me, "After my mama died last year, me and my brother and sister was scared. We didn't know what would happen to us without a mama. But my father got married again right away. A man can't take care of children by hisself, you know. Then our aunt told us, 'Never speak of your mama again. It will make your father feel bad and his new wife uncomfuble.'No one wants to hear you bellyache, so we never talk about it, even with each other. Yeah, it's just the way it is," he concluded. He shrugged his scrawny shoulders in a way that said you couldn't change the past. But he seemed weighed down by sadness.

I understood. Marcella, known as our "old mother" after our Daddy, Glen Cederholm, married Carma, got sick a lot. A headache would put her in bed for the day. When Billy and I said we didn't feel good, she'd give us warm milk or put a cold cloth on our foreheads and lie down with us until we felt better.

My brother and I learned not to bother "new mother" Carma with petty complaints. She would feel our foreheads. If there was no fever, we got a look that said, "I went to nursing school. I've seen people die." Aches and pains? She told us to take an aspirin and lie down. We secretly craved coddling, not time alone in a quiet room.

If I complained of feeling too sick to go to school, Carma felt my forehead. Taking a clothespin from her mouth—she was always hanging up newly washed diapers—she said briskly, "Go to class. If you still feel sick at noon I'll come and get you." Since I was sick at the thought of going to school—dreading a test, having to admit I hadn't done my homework—I was cured once I entered the classroom.

Polio was our worst fear, a lurking terror. Epidemics swept the country. No one knew how to fend it off or how to treat it. Polio could paralyze, put you in braces or even an iron lung for life. The iron lung breathed for you while you lay in a metal cylinder, looking into an overhead mirror to see what was going on around you. There were theories about how polio spread. Was it mosquito-borne? Crop dusting planes drenched communities with DDT to no avail.

Daddy had his own idea. "You kids stop chewing bubble gum," he demanded, his voice tense with worry. "Germs might land on the bubbles, and you'll suck them in and get polio." Billy and I looked at each other, wide-eyed. No more pink Dubble Bubble? We promised we would stop but we knew we wouldn't.

Maybe we should have. On a hot summer day in June, ten-year-old Billy and I came home from swimming at the Star Plunge. Splashing for hours in its heated mineral water had sapped our strength. Billy shuffled into the living room and plopped onto the armless grey davenport we unfolded when visitors needed a place to sleep. His bare feet rested on the flower-patterned linoleum. For once, he didn't grumble that it felt cold. "I'm tired," he complained, "and I have a headache. My back hurts."

I went into the bathroom to towel dry my hair. When I returned, he was sitting in the same place, listless. It wasn't like him to sit quietly; Like Daddy, he jittered with nervous energy. Now Carma leaned anxiously over my brother. She had her hand on his forehead.

"So your legs hurt? And your neck is stiff and you ache all over?" We'd never heard that tone of voice before. She stood up and called sharply, "Glen! Call Dr. Vicklund."

Dr. Vicklund came to our house with his medical bag. He looked worried. We watched as he questioned my brother, turned him over to put a stethoscope on his chest and then on his back. After few minutes of pressing and prodding, he looked up. I was scared when he said, "He should go to the hospital." He never said "polio" but I read it in Daddy's face and in Carma's concerned expression. She was suddenly authoritative. "I want him to have a spinal tap. If it's polio for sure, he needs treatment. If nurses suspect it isn't polio, they'll spend their time with other patients."

The test confirmed the worst. They went to the hospital. I stayed home with two-year-old Jerry and Darcy, just fourteen months old. Daddy and Carma came home anxious, downcast. There were so many polio cases in the small Hot Springs County Memorial Hospital that beds filled the hallways. I heard Carma say dubiously, "They said they'll start treatment as soon as they can, but I don't know. I've never seen the place so busy."

There was a new treatment for polio, she told us, devised by an Australian nurse called Sister Kenney. Doctors had always immobilized polio patients with braces and splints. Sister Kenny's treatment involved application of hot packs and careful movement of affected limbs. Carma had learned about it in nursing school.

The next day they made another visit. Young patients, unattended, were wrapped in wet dressings grown cold. Nurses, whether from overwork or ignorance, weren't doing the treatment correctly. Carma stayed at the hospital when Daddy returned to work. Six months pregnant, leaving her two toddlers in my care, she spent hours at the hospital tending to Billy. He was paralyzed and couldn't move his arms and legs. She soaked wool blankets in the hottest water possible, wrung them out, and applied them to his body before covering him with rubber sheets to keep in the heat. As the blankets cooled, she replaced them with hot ones. She exercised her stepson's limbs as he lay in bed, helpless.

Gramma Cederholm came from Montana to take care of Jerry, Darcy, and me. She was urgently concerned about her oldest grandson. Carma's nursing skills saved Billy from the crippling effects of polio. When he came home he was weak but could walk and move without assistance. He survived. Carma's pregnancy did not. Billy came home but Carma stayed in the hospital. Dr. Vicklund treated her threatened miscarriage by putting her in a hospital bed cranked up at the foot. He hoped by that to stop a too-early birth. Daddy fixed their double bed the same way, using two big blocks of wood. While she lay in that uncomfortable position, her parents came from Burlington, Wyoming, and took Jerry and Darcy home with them. Billy and I went to Montana with Gramma Cederholm.

The bed treatment didn't save the baby. A month later we came home to a smoothly run household. Jerry and Darcy were toddling around. Carma was on her feet again, cooking, cleaning and washing diapers. As she stood at the porcelain sink just drained of hot soapy water, she reached into the cupboard above. A baby bottle fell, crashed into the sink, and splintered into shards. Carma started to sob. Billy and I glanced at her, puzzled but indifferent, and headed out the

door into the sunshine. Like most children, we were monu-
mentally self-centered. It was another malady mineral water
couldn't cure.

When the Road to Health Was Paved with Crisco

By Glennis Cedarholm McNeal

M Y GRAMMA CEDERHOLM WAS KNOWN AS ONE OF THE BEST cooks in Denton, Montana. For a small fee, she boarded teachers at her home during the school year. There were no rental houses or apartments for single people, so unmarried teachers had to live with families who wanted the prestige and the income.

Boarding with families was no bargain. A teacher lost privacy, was subject to insistent matchmaking, and in some cases, deplorable food. There was no other choice for them until Gramma bought the town's only hotel. Two bachelor high school teachers were happy to live there for the school year. The hotel offered relative privacy in gossipy Denton, population 300 and shrinking. In a town this size, even the sidewalks had ears.

Gramma provided more than privacy. She hosted the men each evening at her own table. A typical meal was a thick beef roast browned in Crisco, topped with onion slices and mushroom soup and pressure cooked to tenderness. It glistened with onion/mushroom gravy. The meal included two vegetables, hot yeast rolls, and a casserole of cheese-topped potatoes pulled bubbling from the oven. Canned fruit cocktail encased in shimmering red Jell-O rounded out the menu and our waistlines. The grand finale might be strawberry shortcake served with cream bought from a local farm family. The cream, so thick it held a serving spoon upright, was so delicious I begged for a pint as my birthday gift.

Teachers approached her table with delight and dread. They knew they'd have wonderful food. They feared sinking into a food coma before meal's end. To eat sparingly would insult Gramma, whose reputation as a hostess and a cook was at stake every day at five p.m. Her favorite recipes called for Crisco. Crisco, according to recipe books sponsored by its manufacturer, Procter & Gamble, was superior to butter, lard, and margarine because it was an all-vegetable product. Unlike butter, it didn't need refrigeration because it was hydrogenated. Unlike lard, an animal product that might contain impurities, Crisco came from a factory, not a slaughterhouse. The product was scientifically pure. Crisco cookbooks and cooking shows drove home this point. You could fry with it, bake with it, use it to grease bakeware. It was so pure some women used it as face cream.

Local cooks and bakers believed wholeheartedly. Gramma's cookbook highlighted "Crisco Pie," the crust made with Crisco, not lard. Ingredients for "Crisco Salmon Treat" called for 1-1/2 cups of shredded salmon, ½ cup onion juice, and lemon juice. Blended into a white sauce made of melted Crisco, bread crumbs, milk and eggs, the treat was packed into a loaf pan, chilled, sliced and fried, of course, in Crisco.

Crisco was all-vegetable, gosh darn it. What could be better for you than vegetables and hydrogen?

Gramma had her own recipes, too. Her favorite was "Lemon Luncheon Salad." A six- ounce package of lemon gelatin was dissolved in hot water, then stirred into two cups of mayonnaise. After it chilled to a syrupy consistency, Gramma added chopped celery, canned shrimp and banana slices. It made six servings when poured into a ring mold. In my experience, it served twelve to twenty-four. A glimpse of shrimp and banana in a jiggly yellow ring weakened one's grip on the serving spoon. One tended to take small servings. Very small servings, if one tried it at all.

Gramma fed us physically and emotionally until she had a stroke. Sadly puzzled, I wondered if it was caused by something she ate.

LOUISE MENGELKOCH'S STORIES

Louise Mengelkoch moved to Lake Oswego, Oregon, from Minnesota in 2014. She is a retired journalism professor, with four children and three grandchildren. She lives with her husband, author Kent Nerburn. She is writing a book-length memoir about life as a grandmother.

Deep in the Forest of Our Minds: Goldilocks and Fantastic Beasts

By Louise Mengelkoch

THANKSGIVING 2016

I'M AN UNAPOLOGETIC BOOK ADDICT, AND, LIKE MOST ADDICTS, I enjoy getting others hooked on my drug of choice. Pleasure loves company as much as misery. Back in the '90s, when my youngest child was little, I discovered books on tape, which, to me, are magical. It's like being a child again and having Mom or Dad read to me. Audio books weren't nearly as ubiquitous as they are now, and I had to work hard and pay real money to find appropriate ones for Nik and me to listen to during the many miles we drove on country roads to school, to visit relatives in the big city, or just running errands. The high point of our listening experience was the unabridged version of the first Harry Potter book, which we listened to so many times that Nik recited the first three pages from memory when he auditioned for a major role in a summer stock theater. He landed the role easily.

Since then, I've listened to thousands of hours of books while I drive, take long walks or cook meals. And I've tried to pass on my love of book listening to my grandchildren. All in all, it's been a smashing success. It's challenging when I have both kids in the car at the same time because they are five years apart in age, but we've found some common ground—the "Mrs. Piggle Wiggle" series, any books by Roald Dahl, classic fairy tales and Beatrix Potter stories.

This day I had to pick up five-year-old Thea and take her to my house for the afternoon. I'd just stopped at the library to pick up some of her favorites and some new choices. While I buckled her in her car seat, she perused her options and eventually landed on a curious version of "Goldilocks."

"Okay, Thea," I announced. "Are you ready?" I pushed in the CD as I started the car and she opened her book to the first page. She's learned the routine of turning the page at the special sound. "Once upon a time," it began. This was a rather wry interpretation of the story, and I think that's why Thea liked it so much. Little Goldilocks is portrayed as a "naughty girl" who did whatever she wanted, and that's why she wandered into the forest. After she runs off, the baby bear asks his mother, "Who was that girl anyway?" His mother answers something like, "I don't know but I hope we never see her again!" The story ends, "and they never did."

The story ended just as we arrived at my house. "Do you know what porridge is?" I asked.

"Is it like soup?" she asked. I explained that it was more like hot cereal. "I want some!" she exclaimed. "Will you make me some?"

I got out the box of oatmeal. Then I had a bright idea, which I initially dismissed because I'd hoped to tell Thea to play with her dollhouse so I could spend some time on a calligraphy project. But then I derided myself for my lazy, selfish attitude. "How about if you and I play Goldilocks?" Thea looked puzzled for a few seconds, and then her little face lit up. "Yes!" she said in her wee little voice. We found three bowls from my diverse collection of pottery I'd bought from art students at the college where I used to teach. One was big and dark red. We picked a cobalt blue medium-sized bowl, and a brown little bowl. I put plain oatmeal in the two bigger bowls, but in the little bowl I topped it with raisins and maple syrup. I heated the large bowl in the microwave to make it really hot and put the medium bowl in the freezer for a few minutes.

While we waited, we set three placemats on the dining room table. Then we decided which chairs and beds would be used for the little drama. I set the bowls carefully on the table. "Should we have the Mary doll be Goldilocks?" I asked. Mary was named after my mother, who died long before Thea was even born, but sometimes Thea talks about her almost as if she has some secret connection to her great-grandmother's spirit. During the last couple years of Mary's life, she started collecting stuffed animals and dolls and would sometimes sleep with them. I bought her this rather expensive storybook doll with golden sausage curls for her 90th birthday.

"No," she said decisively. "I want to be Goldilocks." Even though Thea is a brunette, I decided that would work. "Okay," I said. "But then you need to be Baby Bear too." She nodded and we began.

Thea went outside. She rang the doorbell and then knocked. As the narrator, I began by saying loudly, "Goldilocks decided she would come in the house since nobody was home." Thea entered. "Then she walked in and saw three bowls of porridge on the table," I continued. I kept prompting her as she first sat in the chair by the large red bowl. "Goldilocks tried the porridge and said . . . ," I began. I had to feed her the line about it being too hot. She obviously was finding it a challenge to remain in character. Her droll little mouth was drawn up in a bow, but she found the strength to carry on. Mama Bear's was too cold, of course, and then she actually did eat Baby Bear's all up. "That was so good!" she exclaimed, once again out of character, but actually quite apt.

"Then," I continued, "Goldilocks decided to sit down for a while." Thea sat in the chair we'd determined was Papa Bear's—a tall winged-back upholstered in fabric imprinted with pictures of books. "But the chair was too . . . ," I prompted. "Hard!" she said. Mama Bear's chair was a soft leather recliner, clearly too soft. Baby Bear's chair was a sweet little rocker upholstered in cat fabric.

But it was time to move on to the bedroom scene. Since we don't have a room with three beds, we had to move around. Papa Bear's bed was our king-sized bed, clearly perfect for a large bear, and it could be considered a little hard. Mama Bear's bed was the rollaway set up in Kent's basement office, and it actually is a little soft, especially with the memory foam pad on the top. Baby Bear's bed was in our guest room, which doubles as my office. It's appointed with a twin-sized futon, four large containers of Legos and a bookcase filled with kids' books. I helped her curl up and covered her with the soft afghan, which, remarkably, featured a pattern of evergreen trees, deer, moose and bears—a lot of bears. Thea was enchanted. She thought her bed was just right.

So I ended up playing the role of Baby Bear as the three bears wandered back into the house. I had to shout my lines so Goldilocks could hear me from the guest room. When I appeared by her futon and shouted in my best imitation of a wee little bear voice, "And here she is!" Thea jumped up and ran out of the house right on cue.

What a perfect afternoon. We were both pretty pleased with ourselves.

The next day Thea arrived with her nine-year-old brother Truman while Mom went to a physical therapy appointment. I had set out the beautiful German mid-century modern dollhouse on the living room carpet for her. She made a beeline for it, and Truman headed straight for the guest room and the Legos after checking the refrigerator for any contraband items.

He settled on apple cider. I told him I'd make them both a snack in a while. I have learned to hide the TV remotes in my closet, otherwise that's the path of least resistance for us all.

The time flew by. Mom appeared and the kids began putting on their coats. I found myself once again overcoming my laziness and asking if Truman would like to go to the movie with me and if that was alright with Mom. I knew he wanted to see *Fantastic Beasts and Where to Find Them,* and it was playing at my favorite theater, which is within walking distance of our house. They were both enthusiastic.

It wasn't raining as if often does during the fall months in Oregon, so the fifteen-minute walk was easy. We followed the railroad tracks along the lake and ended up almost at the theater. "Wow!" said Truman. "We didn't even have to go on a street or anything!" We loaded up on pizza, red licorice and grape soda and joined all the other kids and parents sitting in the darkened theater on this school holiday just before Thanksgiving.

The movie was delightful. The plot seemed confused to me and I couldn't keep the characters straight, but it didn't matter. The special effects were stunning and the audience was in a festive mood. I made sure to ask Truman a lot of questions based on his knowledge of Harry Potter-inspired magical powers. He was in his element and began offering me tidbits of information without being asked—the difference, say, between a Muggle and a Squib.

On the walk home, we talked about magic, about Harry Potter, about computer-generated images, about what was real and what wasn't. That prompted him to talk about when he discovered that Santa Claus wasn't real. It was just last year, he said, when he saw some message on his mom's cell phone about buying him something that was supposed to be from Santa. "But my sister still thinks he's real," he said. "I don't want to tell her that's he's not."

Like any well-meaning adult, I encouraged him to think of Santa as the spirit of goodwill, but his take was a bit more literal. "I always wondered," he mused, "why everyone thought it was okay that this old guy got to go into everyone's house while they were sleeping. And how did he get all the way around the world in one night? And how could he live at the North Pole?" I allowed as it did beggar the imagination but that logic didn't enter into the equation in any myth or fairy tale. These stories get started because they capture our imagination. We talked about the suspension of disbelief, playfulness and creativity.

So today I'm thinking about those things too, and the difference between the five-year-old mind and the nine-year-old and the sixty-nine-year-old mind. Thea's life is based almost entirely on an imaginary world that is more real to her than what most of us are immersed in every day. Truman is struggling to grow up and feels somewhat betrayed by discovering that things he believed to be literally true are devices to convey emotions, fears, hopes and the search for the beautiful. And where am I on that spectrum? I think I'm struggling to re-enter the realm of the imagination that I seldom entered for a long time. My linear world of responsibilities, deadlines, endless tasks and worries make it seem like an afterthought. But these two days of playtime were more precious than any serious adult task I could have assigned myself. I give thanks on this special day for my unruly, questioning, curious grandchildren.

Election Day Blues

By Louise Mengelkoch

OCTOBER 2016

WHEN I WAS A CHILD IN THE '50S, ELECTION DAY WAS LIKE A holy day of obligation in our family. On those First Tuesdays of November, we would head to our polling place right after Mom and Dad got home from work. Going into that polling booth with one of them was, to me, even more sacred than entering the darkened confessional at church. Then we'd go home and eat TV dinners while we stayed glued to the radio and television awaiting the results. Sometimes it went on late into the night, but I was allowed to stay up as long as it took. Some nights were cause for celebration. Some were not. But it was always thrilling and ceremonial.

Since then, I have become a diligent voter, always keeping up my voter registration and boning up on candidates and issues. I find it dramatic in the same way many people do college and pro sports. Beginning in the early '90s, I had the opportunity to participate in a different way during my career as a journalism professor. I became an academic group leader for a non-profit in Washington, D.C. It was a profound and life-changing experience. I was able to attend political conventions, inaugurations, and spend two weeks in D.C. every January with hundreds of college students.

I was in Mile-High Stadium when Obama gave his acceptance speech. I was hiking through the blizzard in D.C. when Monica Lewinsky was bringing pizza to Bill Clinton. I got to meet senators, congressmen and congresswomen, well-known television journalists and pundits, to sit in the Supreme Court, and attend lavish convention parties for the media. I watched George W. Bush being sworn in. I watched Barack Obama being sworn in. That day I was huddled out in the extreme cold with about a dozen African-American women dressed in their Sunday best—fur coats, high heels and dramatic hats, some of whom had traveled thousands of miles for this historic moment.

We listened on someone's cell phone because we couldn't see or hear from our vantage point. I'd given away my two tickets to some students. I remember all of us crying to think of being witness to this day.

But in some ways, the political activity I value most deeply took place since then. At some point, I was approached to be an election judge in Beltrami County, the remote northern Minnesota area where I had lived and worked for decades. There were about six of us, all women, to handle Turtle Lake Township. I had to report by 6:30 a.m., not my favorite time of day. I drove the winding country road past lakes and woods to the highest point in the county, where I entered a historic one-room schoolhouse with the most beautiful cast-iron heating wood stove I've ever seen. Our toilet needs were served by a sturdy outhouse in the back. The plank floors would squeak as we hurriedly prepared for the arrival of the first voters at seven a.m.

Once the voters arrived, one of us would look up the person's name in the register and have him or her sign in. One of us would hand out a number. One would hand out a ballot. One would register new voters, since Minnesota has an extremely progressive same-day voter registration law. One person, usually our fearless leader, Kris, who worked as a public defender, would deal with complications.

The township clerk would supply us with pizza, sandwiches, and homemade treats. There would definitely be lulls, but at times, we could hardly keep up. This was Minnesota after all, which has the highest voter turnout rate in the country. In 2004, it was 78 percent. It was always so festive, so dreamlike. I almost cry thinking about it. In 2008, my younger son appeared for his first voting experience. He called the setting "iconic" and gave me a big hug when he left. "Good for you Mom!" he said about my volunteer work. When the polls closed at eight p.m., our real work began. We had to add up the votes, double- and triple-check them, put them in a secure box and deliver them to the county courthouse. I would usually get home about ten or eleven p.m. That's a fifteen-hour workday.

Nik was wrong about it being volunteer work. We actually got paid, but it wasn't much. I would use the money for a nice dinner out or some celebratory event.

Now here I am in Oregon, where voting is so easy and

convenient that it's hard to understand how anyone could reasonably not vote. I will mail in my ballot in a few days and spend election day in a faraway city. But it won't feel quite right. There's something about that civic experience that reaffirms the solemnity of the civic responsibility. There is so little ceremony left in my life. As a lapsed Catholic, I don't go to church. Now that I'm retired, I have no academic events such as graduations to attend. Voting day can't replace all that, but it provided me with a grounding that I found nourishing. I miss it.

The Rez School

By Louise Mengelkoch

O N A BITTERLY COLD DAY SOMETIME IN EARLY DECEMBER OF 1971, I stood in a shabby classroom in an old wooden BIA building on a remote Ojibwe Indian reservation awaiting the arrival of my fourteen students—all seventh-grade boys. It was my first day as a language arts teacher and I was quietly terrified. The three tumultuous years I was to spend at Pine Point Experimental School would change my life in so many ways that I can still feel the reverberations to this day.

I wasn't there because of any noble intentions. I wasn't trying to save anybody's soul or mind. I just needed a job and no teachers were being hired in the Twin Cities due to budget cuts. I had completed my student teaching, which was with the problem students in a suburban high school, and my two supervisors liked my spunk. My university adviser liked my journal. He was a published poet and had a poet friend who'd just taken a job as the director of a K-8 school in the village of Ponsford, on the White Earth Reservation in northwestern Minnesota. He got me an interview with one phone call.

My husband and I drove four hours to the White Earth

Reservation, which lies on the eastern edge of the great prairies that stretch across North Dakota and part of Montana and on the western edge of the woodlands that stretch to the Atlantic coast. We camped near Lake Itasca, the source of the Mississippi River, which begins its 2,320-mile journey from there as a tiny rill.

The interview may have been the strangest one I've ever had, and I've had a lot of jobs during my life. I had been given directions to drive to the southeastern corner of the reservation and meet with the school director at his trailer house. It was August and hot and still as only the prairie can be, as if every living thing is hibernating for the rest of the summer. The trailer sat on a newly disturbed plot of land at the northeast corner of two intersecting dirt roads. The forest was visible a ways off, but the house sat vulnerable in the blazing sun.

The inside of the trailer was in distress. Rodger's wife sat silent, almost catatonic, in the living room, while we sat at the kitchen table, on which sat several crates of ripe peaches, a precious commodity this far north.

"Are you going to get to canning these today?" he asked her pointedly, in a tone that made it obvious that he'd been asking that same question for a number of days. At that point, I realized by appearance and smell that the peaches were on the verge of rotting.

She didn't answer.

Rodger asked me a few questions about my teaching philosophy and my experience with minority youth, then drove me in his pickup truck to the maroon and white BIA school building, vintage 1930s. He was a tall, lanky handsome man, in his early thirties, I guessed. His straight black hair was always hanging in his eyes, and he had a way of pushing it back that was extremely attractive. I was enchanted by him and by the raw challenge of teaching in such a school.

When the funding finally came through for my position by Thanksgiving, Rodger's wife had left him, along with his two daughters and moved away. Rodger was by then in a relationship with one of the young white teachers. I remember thinking poorly of his wife at the time, but when I became a mother four years later, I understood her position all too well. Having said that, Rodger and Jane, the young teacher, would later become good friends of ours and we would all live in a sort of commune until things fell apart.

Our moving date was set for December 1st. Jim and I decided to make a road trip to Michigan on Thanksgiving weekend to visit friends from our time living in Germany. Jim had been stationed there in 1969-1970, and we missed our good times and good friends we'd had during that magical experience. When we returned from our weekend trip, however, we found that everything of value had been stolen from our second-floor duplex apartment—all the state-of-the-art electronics we'd bought in Germany; a hand-carved chess set; sporting equipment; even some clothing, including a rather distinctive jacket I'd bought in Germany. We reported it to the police, but to no avail. Then the next day I saw the young woman who lived in the first-floor apartment wearing my jacket. I was so astonished, I didn't know what to do. I was naïve enough to think that if I showed the police a photo of me wearing the jacket, it would prove that she'd stolen it. The perp was probably her shiftless boyfriend, who we'd seen hanging around a lot. She was defiant when I confronted her. The sense of violation was so strong that it made us eager to leave.

I survived that first day of teaching, but I do remember that a twenty-dollar bill was stolen from my purse by the time I left for home. That was real money in those days, especially for a beginning teacher. I believe my salary was about $7,500 for the year, almost exactly what my father earned that same year after almost twenty years as a school bus driver. From then on, I locked up everything, and took to wearing a ring of keys on a macramé rope around my neck, as the other teachers did. The atmosphere at Pine Point was chaotic, creative, magical and tragic. Most of us tried so hard, but the odds were not in our favor. Our school cook made fattening comfort food for both breakfast and lunch, including lovely loaves of aromatic, fluffy white bread, Indian tacos and oatmeal. The kids were smart and dumb, hateful and loving all at once. We lived in a perpetual state of contradictions.

Rodger was the director, but the principal was a tall, ruggedly handsome Ojibwe man named Jerry Buckanaga, who was fresh from a principal licensure program at Harvard. Rodger did the behind-the-scenes work so Jerry could be the charismatic star. They both did their jobs well. Jerry had been an amateur boxer, so he started a boxing program for the kids. He led all the kids and teachers on a one-mile run before we started our lessons each morning. We had family days, family nights, free dinners, anything to get parents involved.

But I had thirteen- and fourteen-year-old boys taller than I was who couldn't read, and at least one who couldn't even make it through the alphabet. It was daunting, to say the least. And some kids ate only what they got at school. Some kids were obviously physically and sexually abused. Some eighth-grade girls were pregnant. Some were addicted to paint-sniffing. I had kids who'd never been in a two-story building or on an escalator or elevator. I took a group to Minneapolis for some kind of field trip and we stayed at a downtown hotel. Two of the boys climbed out the hotel window and started walking along the parapet. We had to talk them down. Kids came to school when it was thirty-five below zero without coats or gloves or hats. They had seen too much and yet were not seen by those whose job it was to care for them. One day, as my husband was waiting in the parking lot to pick me up from work, some guy neither of us even knew drove right into our car for no known reason. It was all perverse and crazy.

It was the closest I've ever come to the kind of experience kids have at summer camp or soldiers have in war. We teachers and Rodger (and sometimes Jerry) spent long hours at work together and socialized together because there was no place to go for entertainment except each other's homes. We were about 30 miles from the nearest small town.

We would cook for each other, drink wine and read poetry and talk about politics and Indian issues. We were on the front lines of the nascent Indian rights movement, and the epicenter was in Minneapolis, where AIM (the American Indian Movement) was founded in 1968 to address the horrors of government termination policies still in effect. Being in the eye of the tornado, we knew less about the big picture than our friends in urban areas watching their TVs and reading major metropolitan newspapers and magazines. When I interviewed for my job, the occupation of Alcatraz had just ended. The "Trail of Broken Treaties" protest in the nation's capital took place a year later, as did the takeover of the BIA building by AIM members. The seventy-one-day armed standoff at Wounded Knee took place in 1973. The ripples from those seismic events streamed into our subconscious. I remember reading an astonishing book called *Bury My Heart at Wounded Knee*, by Dee Brown. It made me angry that I hadn't been taught about these historical events when I was in school. It felt like revolutionary times, especially with the backdrop of increasing anger about the Vietnam War.

I learned all about the BIA and its broken promises, about the horrifying boarding school system. I had the opportunity to observe wild rice being harvested and maple trees being tapped. I learned how to do Indian beadwork and to make frybread. I learned about the reservation where I taught. In 1867, white do-gooders in the Andrew Jackson administration located the 100-square-mile White Earth Reservation in a place where the Indians would have opportunity to hunt, farm and fish because of its varied topography. But the Dawes Act of 1887 made it possible for whites to buy land on the rez, so that it became what is called "checkerboarded." The integrity of the rez was so compromised that it was no longer a unified area. By the 1970s, the only employment available on the rez was the school. Everything had already been logged off the land, and fishing was not a viable way to make a living. Needless to say, the only farmers were white. Even then, it was subsistence farming. The only other place of employment of which I was aware was, of all things, a puzzle factory.

In 1982, a young Jewish-Ojibwe woman by the name of Winona LaDuke would move to her grandparents' home on White Earth and form the White Earth Land Recovery Project to buy back as much of the lost land as possible. Winona would become Ralph Nader's running mate in the 1996 and 2000 presidential elections. She also became a colleague of mine at Bemidji State University and I team-taught environmental studies courses with her.

The three years I spent at Pine Point was one of the most stimulating times of my life. I didn't feel so much like a naïve young thing who was shocked into awareness, but like someone who'd finally found her intellectual, political and cultural soulmates. It's difficult to explain, but despite all the craziness and hardship, I felt challenged and, to a certain point, up to the task. I grew up. I also learned a lot about the complications of adult life. I had friends who were going through divorces. My own marriage was becoming shaky.

Jim had been kind of at loose ends ever since he was discharged from the army in the summer of 1970. While I was busy finishing my degree in English education, I have no memory of what Jim was doing. When we moved to the rez, he enrolled as an undergraduate student at Bemidji State University with a major in industrial education. He'd started college before he was drafted, but flunked out. Now, with the help of the generous GI Bill and my full-time salary, it seemed like the right time. It was a fifty-mile drive each way to the campus, but it was common (and still is) for rural students to travel even farther for a college education so they don't have to relocate.

My first hint that things were not right came early on. I

arrived home early one spring day in 1972. Jim was home. He had an explanation that in retrospect was inadequate, but at the time, I believed him. It was something about all his classes being cancelled. At some point, I must have opened the mail before he saw it and discovered that he'd flunked all his courses.

The next fall, the school director and, by now, our good friend, Rodger, hired Jim at the school to build a multi-level structure with little cubbies for my students so they could each have their own study carrel. It took up most of my classroom, and, as I could have predicted, did not aid in their academic accomplishments. But it was impressive, and, of course, the kids loved it.

Whites were not allowed to live on the rez, so most of us lived in makeshift housing five to ten miles from the school. That first year, Jim and I lived in a cabin on Shell Lake. The heating system was so inadequate that the entire front of the cabin frosted up on the inside during the weeks when it would get to thirty-five or even forty below zero at night. We spent more on heat than we did on rent. We had to move out by the fishing opener in early May because the resort owner could make more income by renting out his cabins for a weekend than he could from us in a month. We found a crumbling yellow frame cabin on Boot Lake for the summer, which was unrentable to vacationers because of its condition. My sister-in-law crashed through the floor one day simply walking across the room. We could see the ground. We got ringworm from sitting on the sandy beach.

There was one white couple who did live on the rez—in fact, within sight of the school. John and Kathy somehow were able to rent the former rectory next to the Catholic church. John was our physical education teacher and Kathy was a housewife in an era when it was becoming an endangered species. They had met somewhere in South America in the Peace Corps, and after they married went off to Iran to teach. So they had stories to tell. Jim and I became close friends with them, and we stayed in contact long after we all left Pine Point. It must have been a strange life for them in that old stark white house within full view of everyone in the tiny settlement of Ponsford—not even any trees for privacy. It was just plain weird.

I remember Kathy hanging out her laundry on Mondays and having to watch it dry because kids were too tempted to steal it or muddy it up a bit. On Tuesdays, of course, she ironed. She made me think of the pioneer wives who continued the hopeless mission of trying to continue their so-called civilized life in totally inappropriate places for no reason. Years later, she and John would adopt two South American children who got to know my own children when we would visit them in Iowa, where John studied for his doctorate in education.

Within sight of John and Kathy's house lived a reclusive elderly white couple who sold colorful Czech glass beads, which were wildly popular with anyone who made pow-wow garb. Their custom-built log home was filled with Indian artifacts. It was a miracle that nothing was ever stolen. But a miracle would also be needed to save her from the cancer that killed her. I heard that she was resistant to seeking medical help, and the tumor in her breast actually broke open. Probably just a story, but those were the kind of dark rumors that spread like wildfire on the rez.

The school staff was mostly young, creative, energetic and visionary. There was Lynn, a beautiful sweet young woman with long blonde hair, who lived alone and ate brown rice and vegetables. Jane, Rodger's girlfriend, was an energetic and ambitious farm girl from a large family in North Dakota. Tom was a small-town, unprepossessing young man who was an absolute saint. He later married Beeb, one of the teachers' aides and the two of them taught at the school together for many years after the rest of us left. The aides were all Ojibwe from the rez. One of them, Erma Vizenor, would later earn a college degree and become the first woman to be elected tribal chairperson. Jane and Rodger eventually married. Jane became a community college president and Rodger became a full-time poet, consultant and grant-writer. Jerry Buckanaga became an Indian studies instructor at the University of Minnesota. He died at age fifty-five of a heart attack. I believe one of his sons was murdered. They were all such handsome, talented, kind people. It was tragic.

John and Kathy would eventually move to Bemidji, about fifty miles northeast of Ponsford, where I also ended up decades later. He became the principal of the Red Lake Reservation high school and hired my second husband to head an oral history project in 1988. As for me, my first master's thesis was on the Native American novel. I ended up back in Indian country in 1987 when I was hired to edit a newspaper for the Red Lake Reservation. Eighteen years later, Red Lake High School would be the scene of a horrific school shooting that left eight people dead and five wounded. But that's another story.

There was at least one teacher who was not like the rest of us. Malvina just didn't fit in. She used hairspray and wore dresses. She was close to retirement and had to hang in there for a while, but she would have been more comfortable in an old mission boarding school than an experimental school. Malvina was our only special education teacher, and most of my students were tutored by her for an hour or more each week. One of my boys freaked her out when he decided he'd had enough tutoring and jumped out the window. Now that I'm older than Malvina was at that time, I have some degree of sympathy for her. She probably couldn't get a transfer to another school, so she was trapped.

In the fall of 1972, Jim and I moved to an old white two-story farmhouse in Osage, an unincorporated township of several hundred people with a white frame Lutheran church and a tiny café. The house boasted a beautiful oversized pink enamel cook-stove in the kitchen, in addition to a 1950s-era electric stove. My commute was nine miles on a narrow two-lane rural road that zig-zagged back and forth along section lines. This was the year Jim worked at the school, so we would ride together. I remember making professional improvement trips to other Indian schools in the state and learned so much about Indian education, Minnesota geography and history, but none of it made much difference on a day-to-day basis with our students. While we teachers and administrators were gaining knowledge and experience and would move on to other things, the children continued to suffer.

But Jerry, our principal, had an idea. Towards the end of the 1972-1973 school year, he found a way to break off from the Park Rapids School District, which was based in a racist resort town about twenty miles south of Pine Point. He also determined that there were enough qualified Indian teachers available to replace all the non-Indian teachers. It may have been a good idea, but he was mistaken in his assumption about the availability of native teachers. We would be tapped again for help. When we all received our walking papers sometime that spring, a few of us had an idea, spearheaded by Rodger. We found an opportunity to lease the land surrounding an entire lake near Itasca Park. Our dream was to start an outdoor education center and live communally. We followed our dream, which soon turned into a nightmare. But that's another story.

The lessons I took away from that dramatic period were not pleasant ones. I learned that some historic tragedies are so great and the fallout so complex that they take centuries to resolve, if ever. I learned that it's possible to not particularly like contemporary manifestations of a culture but still appreciate and respect the historical tradition. I learned to not take everything personally, but at the same time realize an individual is capable of good and also harm. And finally, I can't deny the unseen forces that were both irresistible and disconcerting—a people and culture older and more deeply embedded in the land than anything I had experienced as the great-grandchild of European immigrants whose history and origins were an ocean away and lost to me. It made me realize that they are the rightful heirs to the land on which I live and that I and my descendants will never be their equal. In short, I learned about original sin and how difficult it is for Americans to make their peace with it.

NANCY MURRAY'S STORY

Nancy Murray, seventy-two, was born and raised in California, but spent almost all her adult years in Oregon. Travel continues to be an education and a true pleasure as well. She stands almost alone at not minding airports or airplanes, because they take her to interesting places and bring her home again.

Bed and Breakfasts and Other Cultural Treasures to Discover

By Nancy Murray

M Y HUSBAND AND I HAD SPENT OUR FIRST TWO YEARS OF MAR-
riage in two very quiet cities in southern California: San
Luis Obispo and Santa Maria. Santa Maria had so little going
for it that our week's social highlight was happy hour at a restaurant we liked because of its substantial appetizers. After a
while, it occurred to us that we could do better.

One night we began to talk about other job opportunities
with Xerox, Ken's employer of almost three years. The sister
company, Rank Xerox, headquartered in London, had offices
all around the world. Ken had never traveled outside California, and his brush with foreign travel was reading my letters
during my travel days in the Pacific with Pan Am. We set
off for the library, weighed different possibilities, and ended
up choosing London, for the language and better employment
possibilities. We quit our jobs at the end of my teaching year,
put our belongings in storage, packed two suitcases and a
trunk for sending later and set off on our big adventure.

A lot of Americans traveled to Europe during the 1960s, but even by 1970, it was not yet overrun by American tourists. Arthur Frommer had written a popular book called *Europe on $5 a Day*. We took that book, along with our AAA maps, left a typed itinerary with Thomas Cook addresses for parents and friends, and purchased travelers cheques to last us the two months we planned to spend touring London, France, Italy, and little pieces of Austria, Switzerland, Germany, the Netherlands, and Belgium. We'd paid for delivery of our new Volvo sedan from Sweden to London.

But first we needed to go to London to get that job that would allow us to live there. Frommer's $5-a-day guide became our bible. We had never stayed in a bed and breakfast before, only hotels, so they sounded romantic, cultural, and cozy. We secured a room in London for the first night by writing ahead from the U.S., wanting to be sure we wouldn't be wandering streets looking for a vacancy during high tourist season. This was long before fax machines and multiple guide books for economy travelers. We arrived at our first stop to find a small, clean, and comfortable room, but it was too expensive to spend our entire week in London there.

After a greasy "English breakfast" of fried eggs, fried potatoes, canned baked beans, broiled tomatoes, room-temperature dry toast, tasty sausage, and, of course, tea, we set out to find a cheaper room. Using the British public phones in their iconic sidewalk red booths where you had to shove in exact change when you heard the "pips" was very stressful and took a lot of coins, so we knocked on bed and breakfast doors instead. We remained in the Paddington area and looked for vacancy signs. At one we were greeted by an Indian proprietor who had an affordable room. We took it and came back later with our suitcases. Though the hotel foyer was all decked out, our room was just clean enough not to change our minds. We set out to fill the rest of the day with sightseeing, using the

Underground with all its soot and dirt and noise. But, oh, this was so exciting!

That night we needed a good wash. There was one communal bath, and we kept peeking out our door to see when it was available. We decided to wait in the hall so no one else would queue up in front of us. We stood there with towels and bedclothes, soap and shampoo in hand for the longest time, when finally, the door opened. Out stepped a woman in a flowing magenta sari. Following her was a cloud of steam replete with body odor strong enough to take your breath away. We decided to wait for the bathroom to cool down and clear out a bit of the odorous steam cloud. We stepped in to see a tub with a ring around it that was at the very least off-putting. There was no cleaning powder such as Ajax in sight.

Ken went back to our room and got a drinking glass, and we decided to take a stand-up bath. One of us would pour water over the other while the other soaped up and shampooed, then do the rinsing process, step out and help the other get washed up. After a good laugh, we determined this surely was not suitable for the whole week, so the next morning we set off to find another bed and breakfast.

Before we agreed to pay for our stay at our next prospective B&B, we asked to see the bathroom. Our stay there was lovely, and the owners could not have been more accommodating hosts. We saw the sights of London, the crown jewels, ate cheap but delicious curry dinners, and most importantly, got that sales position at Rank Xerox. We were now free to pick up our car and leave for the continent, picking up the work visa in Belgium at the end of our tour to re-enter England with the proper paperwork. We said a warm good-bye to our hosts, but we would see them again.

Five months later, we were to leave London for Ken's new assignment in Tehran, Iran, opening a new sales office there. We needed a night at a bed and breakfast before our morning flight. I called the nice English couple and booked a room.

When we arrived at their front step, the couple answered the door together and gave us a big look of recognition. The wife said to her husband, "Oh, look! It's the American couple who wanted to see the bathroom!"

It was now time to set off for the continent. To prepare for driving in the big cities of Europe, we had helpful AAA maps with directions on how to enter and exit London, Paris and Rome. This saved our marriage several times, since navigating unknown territory with a spouse is often perilous. Leaving London with its left-hand drive on unfamiliar roads and highways called for drastic measures, so we left before dawn with practically no one sharing the road. It was smooth sailing all the way from the B&B to Dover where we caught a ferry across the English Channel to Calais, France.

Looking back, I can still feel the thrill of choosing our own adventure and starring in it, too. We were on our own, fully adult to make our own decisions and our way in the world. Every day so far had brought challenges and delights with the promise of many more to come.

TERRIE OLDHAM'S STORIES

Terrie Oldham grew up in North Dakota and Alaska and Oregon during the '40s and '50s while her father followed his dreams. She worked as a registered nurse for twenty-four years in acute care, education, and administration. Following her nursing career, she opened, owned, and managed a school of floral design, then became a builder/developer, which was her favorite career. She has two children and three grandchildren. She currently has her own small business, "Pamper My Feet," working one to two days a week. She sings in a 100-voice church choir; and she keeps her hands and mind busy with knitting, Chinese brush-stroke painting, creating jewelry, doing crossword puzzles, reading, or just gazing out the window watching the birds.

Cheating and Lies

By Terrie Oldham

WHILE I WAS HOME FROM SCHOOL THAT MONTH ON FORCED leave from nursing school due to my youthful escapades, I worked at my old job cleaning at the Odd Fellows Home. The money was welcome! And yes, I did pass my exams after I returned to Portland, but how I managed to do that, I'm ashamed to tell.

I was always a good student, and I never needed or had a desire to cheat. I knew that, had I been present for the classes, I would have done well on the tests. Well, at least that was my rationalization for my actions. I wasn't about to flunk my first-term exams, so what should I do? Some of my friends and I decided that I needed a copy of the tests, and we had a good idea where they were kept—in that same classroom where we had snuck in the window on our earlier escapade. So one night I quietly crept down to that classroom, found the unlocked drawer where the tests were kept and quickly and diligently took extensive notes. I did do well on the tests and none of my instructors or classmates ever questioned me. That was the first and only time I ever cheated.

There were features of nursing school that I enjoyed—for example, surgery and obstetrics and certainly, being with my friends. But on the whole, I can't say that I really enjoyed much else, at least not the patient care part. None of my friends thought I would stick it out, but I'm not a quitter; I generally finish what I start, and, of course, had to prove them wrong. Besides, what were my other options? Home economics? Secretarial school? Teaching? None of those appealed to me and there weren't that many options for a girl in the 1950s, at least not at Walla Walla College. Also, I didn't want to disappoint my mother. I had always planned on going to college to get a degree, and I was the only one in my family to do so.

Other aspects of being there with my friends made the experience tolerable and fun at times. Sometimes on weekends, we would sign out to one of our "relatives," then walk down the hill about a mile and a half to the Bagdad Theater to see a movie. We didn't know that one of our instructors lived in an apartment very near the theater. We learned that one time by accident. We had to duck behind a building so she wouldn't see us because we weren't allowed to go to movies and we weren't where we said we were going.

We kept a watchful eye out for her thereafter. Then there was the time Donna and Joyce and I signed out for the weekend and went to the beach with our boyfriends. And the time Viola and I wanted to watch the Rose Parade so we stayed overnight with a guy and his buddy she knew who had an apartment near the parade route. Since we had an idea what kind of housekeepers single guys were, we took our own sheets, as we were determined to sleep on the fold-out sofa, much to the guys' disappointment.

There were three black female students in my class. That is of note because WWC School of Nursing had never admitted any black students before. This was the '50s, and segregation was still quite prevalent, at least in Walla Walla. The three of them roomed together; however, I did room with one of them during my senior year for a bit between rotations. One of the girls dropped out, one of them finished, and what happened to the other one was amazing to me!

It was during our surgical rotation when I noticed that Japhena looked different in her scrub uniform. I remember nudging my friends during worship and saying, "Look at Japhena. Don't you think she looks pregnant?" No one else ever said a word about it. We knew she had a boyfriend from Fort Lewis who came to see her frequently. Well, without anyone detecting her condition (except possibly her roommates) she went into labor one day. She was taken to the hospital and delivered a full-term baby boy.

Japhena told the supervisor that she was secretly married to this soldier, so the supervisor called the army base and told the officer she needed to speak with this man because his wife had just given birth to a baby boy. The officer said, "No, I don't think so. I just saw him walking across the grounds with his wife." Poor Japhena! She had no idea he was married. Needless to say, that was the end of her nursing school experience, at least for then. She did go back and finish after she had married and raised her children. She was a lovely young woman.

I was in my last six months of nursing school on my psychiatric rotation at the state hospital in Salem when I got into trouble for the last time and nearly got kicked out of WWC. I really knew how to time these escapades! Viola, Donna and Joyce were in the class six months ahead of me, so they were back on the college campus in College Place finishing up. Anyway, I went home for the weekend. It was Halloween and we were invited to a barn party out in the country. I won't go into detail, but there was alcohol, boys, and a stool pigeon involved. When I went back to Salem, I got a call from Donna telling me the girls' dean there had called them in and questioned them about our party and that she was on her way to Salem to see me. They said they denied that there was alcohol or any other unsanctioned activity at that party and that I should too. The dean arrived, along with the dean of the school of nursing and interrogated me for what seemed like hours.

Naturally, I denied any knowledge of alcohol. (In fact, I had gotten so drunk that I was sick and spent most of the evening lying down on the seat of my date's car to keep from spinning off.) The girls' dean insisted my friends had admitted everything. I knew she was lying because my friends would not lie to me. We probably would have gotten expelled except that Donna's father was a large financial contributor to the college and threatened to withhold any further contributions if we were expelled. So we were all put on probation for three months. What that consisted of for me, since I was in Salem and, after that, on my pediatric rotation at Doernbecher Hospital, was calling the dean of the school of nursing in Portland weekly and reporting in. She was a kind, reasonable woman and never accusatory. So that was a pretty painless punishment.

Looking back on my experiences, I have mixed feelings. I can't say I regret any of them. However, I was attending a school that had certain restrictions and I should have respected them. The lying was out of character for me and certainly not the actions of a Christian. I was young and not seriously considering my spiritual condition then. I regret the lies I told. On the other hand, I was able to finish my schooling because of them.

One Dark Day

By Terrie Oldham

THE NEWLY MANUFACTURED FIBERGLASS OUTBOARD MOTORBOATS seemed like the answer to the loggers' dreams on Vank Island, Alaska. No longer did they worry about the tide going out and leaving their heavy wooden boats stranded on the rocky beach; these new boats were light enough to easily drag down to the water when the tide went out. But on this Sunday, May 20, 1951, one of those light boats proved to be deadly.

The day had turned dark, stormy, and windy, with heavy rain—too nasty to continue working. All agreed it was better to knock off early and head for home, which was just on the other side of the island from where they were logging. So the four-man crew, including my dad, who didn't know how to swim, his brother Uncle Windy, and two other men climbed into the boat with their heavy cork boots laced up to their knees and started for home. The sea became wild, with waves higher than the boat carrying those four men, who wore no life jackets. After all, this was the only mode of transportation for us all. There were no cars or trucks on this small island, so we didn't generally wear life jackets.

The sea was so rough and the waves so high that the light-weight boat capsized and the four clung desperately to the boat, but they weren't worried because they were in sight of the tugboat, the Margie Ann. But the skipper, who was known to drink on the job, hadn't even seen the outboard motor boat being tossed violently around on the stormy sea and struggling to stay afloat. The Margie Ann needed deeper water, so it pitched and rolled along on the swells much further out on the bay.

The loggers usually got home before the tugboat that accompanied them daily to tow the logs back to camp since they were in a smaller boat and could travel faster. Because of that, it wasn't until the tugboat arrived back at camp that the skipper learned that the loggers had not yet returned. At that point, alarm and fear gripped our hearts.

One of the men, Willis Hanson, said he tired of hanging on to the upturned boat in the frigid water so he swam to shore and walked barefoot for 45 minutes on the rocky beach to our camp. He was the sole survivor and the only single man in the group. A search plane was sent from Petersburg and searched all afternoon and into the night, along with other men and boats from Vank Island, including the skipper, Henry Bradley.

My most vivid memory of that dark day is of my mother standing watching at the window for the search plane to come in, filled with hope, then sinking down on the couch, wailing with despair when the report came each time that they had spotted nothing. The plane just kept going out and coming back repeatedly, but it failed to find any trace of the men or the boat. The boat was finally located by Uncle Art, Daddy's younger brother, late that night about twelve miles from the scene of the accident. None of the bodies was ever found, only my dad's black lunch pail and a cap. He was thirty-eight years old.

I have often wondered what his last thoughts would have been. Being that he was a devout Christian, I'm certain he was crying out to God to save them, but also so worried about the family he would leave behind—his thirty-six-year-old wife with four children, ages fourteen, twelve, three and one. He who had wanted a boy so badly when I was born (Terry Daniel, not Terrie Danielle as I was named when I turned out to be a girl) was not going to be around to play with his sons or enjoy seeing them grow up.

A memorial service was held in Wrangell at the Presbyterian church. Stores and businesses were closed during the service in tribute to the three men who drowned. They were "well known and popular in this area," according to the Wrangell Sentinel.

My dad's death did not seem real to me as a twelve-year-old, and I could not grieve. I remember feeling like I should cry because others were, and I tried, but I was unable to. I felt guilty that the last words I had said about my father were, "He makes me so mad I could spit!" The previous day, we had gone into Wrangell to church and he made us wear those horrible tan, knit long stockings that bagged at the knees and ankles. They were ugly—no lycra or pretty colors then—and you had to wear a garter belt to hold them up. I hated them!

Gail, at the age of fourteen, assumed the responsibility of writing to friends and family to let them know of the tragic accident. Mother, who never liked to write letters anyway, was too distraught and had much on her mind with two babies to care for and the worry of how to provide for her family without my dad.

I was haunted for years by the sound of airplanes overhead. And I have often dreamed that my dad is still alive. He just comes walking out of the woods or from somewhere. I would have liked to have gotten to know my father better and I do so look forward to meeting him again in heaven one day!

DAVID PANGBURN'S STORIES

David Pangburn lives in Lake Oswego, Oregon, with his wife Dorris, and his daughter and her two teenage children. He is a retired information technology professional. His education includes an undergraduate degree in business administration and a graduate degree in global business management. He is also a certified business continuity professional. He writes as a hobby, including essays, short stories, novels, and memoirs. He has studied several foreign languages and is widely traveled, taking "the road less traveled" whenever possible.

Stranded in Afghanistan

By David A. Pangburn

IN JANUARY OF 1977, I LEFT TEHRAN, IRAN, WITH MY WIFE AND three-and-one-half- year-old daughter and returned home to Phoenix, Arizona. We'd been in Iran only one year, but our daughter was having problems with epilepsy, so I was permitted to break my two-year contract with ISIRAN, the computer company linked to the Shah of Iran.

I was never happy working and living in Iran for many reasons, so I was happy to leave. So many expatriates had become dissatisfied with the working and living conditions there and had left the country prematurely that the company instituted an incentive program whereby a percentage of the monthly salary was withheld. The only way to collect the withholding was to complete the two-year commitment. In my case, eight-hundred dollars was withheld each month. Fortunately, I was able to collect the nearly ten thousand dollars owed me because of our daughter's need to return to the States.

While in Tehran, I'd met a woman whose husband held some diplomatic position with the U.S. Embassy in Kabul, Afghanistan. She had traveled with two small children by bus from Kabul to the Iranian border, crossed over and then traveled to Tehran by train. I found that to be bold and daring, especially with small children.

She encouraged me to read *Caravans* by James Michener. Published in 1963, it is a story about an American diplomat who was sent to find a woman who had married an Afghan and then disappeared, swallowed up by the Afghan culture. Michener surely must have lived in Afghanistan, because when I arrived in Kabul and traveled to Pakistan, what I witnessed was nearly the same as described by Michener. Everything was so familiar that I thought I had read a Fodor's travel guide instead of a novel. The Afghanistan of 1947 that Michener wrote about was backward and primitive and it was still that way when I visited in 1977—and probably still is today.

The company agreed to pay return fare to the U.S. if we were to return via the same European route as when we arrived. However, we decided that we wanted to see this place called Afghanistan and return to the U.S. via south Asia, even though it would cost us for the additional transportation and lodging. Our itinerary called for a stopover in Kabul before heading to Karachi, Pakistan, with a transfer in Peshawar, Pakistan. For the next three weeks, we would have stopovers in Colombo, Sri Lanka, and Bangkok. As it turned out, we also had stopovers in Hong Kong, Japan, and Hawaii. It was a harried but worthwhile three-week journey with lots of mishaps along the way, but that's another story.

We checked into an inexpensive hotel in Kabul that was once the British officers' barracks, across from the main bazaar. The first thing I did was go to the airline office to check on our flight to Peshawar. I was concerned because the flight between Peshawar and Karachi ran only twice a week and I wanted to ensure that our reservations for the flight were in order. To my surprise, I was told that all airline service between Afghanistan and Pakistan had been suspended two years earlier! Once again, Iran Air had screwed us. They had done it once before and gotten us stranded in Kuwait. But that's another story.

My first impression of Afghanistan was that it didn't even rise to the level of a third-world country. It had been ravaged by many regional wars in the past and soon Russia would be adding to the destruction. There were no railroads in this poor, Texas-sized central Asian country back then. Successive Afghan governments discouraged the construction of railways that could aid foreign interference in Afghanistan by Britain or Russia. Foreigners had, however, built the country's 1,200 miles of paved roads. Besides airline service in the major cities, the only other transportation was by bus. I'm not talking about the big air-conditioned busses we are accustomed to here in the U.S. These busses were old and rickety. I doubt that they could pass vehicle safety inspection here. Luggage was piled atop the bus and the seats were hard.

I was able to secure tickets for one such bus traveling between Kabul and Peshawar. According to the schedule, we should have been able to make it to the airport in Peshawar in time for our flight to Karachi. Since we had a couple of free days before the bus trip, we hired a car and an English-speaking driver and toured Kabul and the surrounding area. In truth, besides the animal bazaar and rundown museum and the sparsely populated zoo, there wasn't much to see or do. The highlight of the animal bazaar was a man riding a bicycle while leading a camel.

Unfortunately, that picture somehow got ruined during film processing when I got home. The bazaar next to our hotel bustled with activity from very early morning until late into the evening, and it was interesting to visit all the merchants and see all the products for sale. I bought a prayer rug, which we lugged all the way back home.

On the morning of departure day, we boarded the bus for the 142-mile trip to Peshawar. It was cold and the bus had no heat. The nearby Hindu Kush Mountains wore a heavy blanket of snow and it started snowing in Kabul as we left. Besides a couple of American students traveling the world, the other passengers were either Afghans or Pakistanis. After a few hours on a high, treeless plateau, the bus dropped off into a precipitous canyon and into Afghanistan's fourth largest city, Jalalabad, surrounded by palm trees and citrus groves and acres of planted fields (probably opium poppies).

I learned later that the road between Jalalabad and Kabul was considered one of the most dangerous in the world, not only because the road conditions were treacherous but also because the people drove recklessly. I can't help but wonder what we would have done if we had known that—returned to Iran, or skipped Karachi and tried to fly directly to Colombo, Sri Lanka, which was also on our travel itinerary? Once I discovered that we could travel to Peshawar by bus, I had discounted all other options.

They drive on the right in Afghanistan and on the left in Pakistan so the bus had two drivers, one of whom spoke English. I guessed that he was from Pakistan and would drive after we crossed the border. After leaving Jalalabad, the bus continued to the border town of Torkham, where Afghanistan closed the border after each country accused the other of providing safe haven for militants. Thankfully, the border was not closed when we got there.

When we arrived at Torkham, there was a lot of confusion and a lot of pushing and shoving as people tried to get processed so that they could cross the border in both directions. I approached the English-speaking driver and tried to impress upon him how important it was that we got Peshawar by five p.m. to catch our plane to Karachi. I even offered each driver twenty U.S. dollars if they could get us there in time. "Give me your passports and wait here," he told me. We complied and he disappeared, leaving me with a sunken feeling. "What have I done, giving away our passports?" I asked myself.

There we were, halfway around the world in a

semiautonomous region controlled by smugglers and militants. I suppose we could go back to the American Embassy in Kabul and try to get new passports. All we could do was sit on the bus and wait. After what seemed like an eternity, he came back and gave us our passports with the Pakistani stamp in them and I gave him two U.S. twenty-dollar bills. Pretty soon the rest of the passengers boarded the bus and we passed into Pakistan and through the famed Khyber Pass, and on to Peshawar, albeit on the other side of the road. The driver must have really wanted that twenty dollars, as evidenced by the way he drove. Perhaps he always drove that fast. All I wanted to do is get us to Peshawar—alive and on time. At last we made it.

I can't help but wonder what the other passengers would have done to me if they had known that their lives were jeopardized by a wild driver because I had paid him to speed up so I wouldn't miss my plane in Peshawar.

Conquering the Mountain

By David Pangburn

I N 1976, I WAS LIVING IN TEHRAN, IRAN. THE CITY LIES ON THE southern slope of the 14,000-ft. Alborz mountain range. About one hundred miles east of Tehran looms an 18,600-ft. dormant volcano called Mt. Damavand. In October of that year I was invited to climb to the top of Mt. Damavand with a group of ex-pats living in Tehran. Being ever ready for an adventure, I agreed to go.

Because Mt. Damavand is a dormant volcano, it constantly spews sulfur gases from its summit. Sunlight reacts with the sulfur compounds and produces a toxic substance. For this reason, the mountain is always climbed at night and climbers reaching the summit do not remain very long after sunrise. Our group hiked up a trail in the daylight from a remote village situated at the 7,000-ft. level up to a mountaineering shelter at the 14,000-ft. level and rested until about midnight, when the moon would be full. Surprisingly, in the rare air and cloudless night at that altitude, the moon shone almost as brightly as stadium lights. Reaching the summit of Mt.

Damavand does not require technical climbing because there is a trail up to the summit from the mountaineering shelter.

At midnight we set out under a bright moon. At about 16,000 ft., I started experiencing altitude sickness and despite my internal objections, I convinced myself to go back down to the shelter. I resolved that I would do the climb in November during the next full moon. Unfortunately, by the next full moon, winter had arrived and the snow level was down to about 4,000 ft. I would have to wait until spring. However, my young daughter got sick and couldn't be treated in Iran, so three months later we returned to the U.S. The mountain would have to wait.

For me, Mt. Damavand has always been a symbol of quitting. That I gave up so easily has always hung over me like the Sword of Damocles. I promised myself that I would one day return to Iran and conquer the mountain. Unfortunately, the Islamic revolution in 1979 dashed those hopes. Even if I could get permission to go to Iran and climb Mt. Damavand today, I'm not so sure, more than forty years later, that I could do the climb because of my age.

On November 22, 2014, I climbed another mountain—metaphorically. I successfully completed my testing for the coveted black belt in the Korean martial arts of Tae Kwon Do. The following is a speech I gave at the ceremony. It basically describes my struggle, as a senior citizen, to obtain the black belt. The theme of the speech was about not quitting and winning through perseverance.

Some of what our Tae Kwon Do Masters teach us what is called the "Five Tenets" of Tae Kwon Do. They are:

- Courtesy
- Integrity
- Self-Control
- Indomitable Spirit

Most of these are self-explanatory but the one that I want to specifically talk about is the fifth one, the one Koreans call *In Nae* (인내):

- Perseverance

Determination is a synonym for *perseverance.* We all know that determination means setting a goal and focusing on it with firmness of purpose, but *perseverance* means continuing to do those things in spite of difficulties and obstacles. All the individuals taking the black belt exam have demonstrated determination and *perseverance.* Their journey to this place has required setting a goal and pursuing it fully. Getting the black belt has been a long, personal journey, one that has meant something different to each one of us.

Mine has been a journey along a very bumpy road, with some mishaps along the way. I want to mention a couple of these because they were sufficient enough for me to want to quit Tae Kwon Do altogether. Some of you at the State Street dojang in Lake Oswego may remember one embarrassing situation that occurred back in 2011 when I first started taking Tae Kwon Do. Some of you may have heard about it. I was running backwards during one of the exercises, lost my balance and fell into the wall—literally *into* the wall—and *through* the wallboard! Fortunately, I hit the wall between the underlying studs, and the only thing I suffered was a bruised ego. At that point, I figured that I would be invited to *not* continue taking Tae Kwon Do!

I could have quit at that point and salvaged my pride but I didn't. Neither was I asked to stop taking Tae Kwon Do. My offer to pay for the repairs was refused so I didn't quit and I *persevered* and continued the training, albeit with some concerns about what calamity might happen next.

My first color belt test a couple months later would be the defining moment. When I passed the test, I was greatly encouraged and was determined to stay the course to earn the coveted black belt, even though that opportunity would be three years away. I knew that a lot can happen in three years, but I *persevered*.

The following year I suffered a serious medical crisis—a heart attack—and had to have a quadruple by-pass operation.

I want to pause here and state that Tae Kwon Do was *not* the cause of the heart attack. I have a family history of heart problems. In fact, I had seven coronary stents before I started taking Tae Kwon Do, but I felt well enough that I didn't consider the physical requirements of Tae Kwon Do to be a health risk. I thought my discomfort was merely indigestion and was treating it as such. This turns out to be a common mistake made by many people with a heart condition. However, the cardiac surgeon attributed the successful surgery and recovery to the fact that Tae Kwon Do had made my body strong, a very important factor for a man of my age.

Here again, this would have been an excellent opportunity to stop taking Tae Kwon Do and nobody could call me a quitter! My four-month recovery progressed well enough that I was able to *persevere* and resume Tae Kwon Do training.

There have been other health-related bumps in the road since then and lots of aches and pains but nothing as dramatic as the heart surgery. The following year, a bout with atrial fibrillation (Afib) almost sidelined my Tae Kwon Do ambitions, but once again I *persevered* and was able to get it controlled with medications.

Because my determination was firm, and my *perseverance* never wavered, I am proud to be standing here today receiving my black belt at the age of 75! Tae Kwon Do has taught me a lot. It has trained my mind and conditioned my body. It has taught me to focus on a goal, and to *persevere* and achieve that goal.

I would encourage all the adults here today—whether you are twenty-five, forty-five, or even sixty-five—to stop by your local Tae Kwon Do dojang and join us. You'll have fun and gain health benefits along the way. You too could be down here on the floor like us, feeling as proud as we are. And besides, it's probably a lot cheaper and more fun than going to the fitness gym—and there's no waiting in line for a machine or a trainer.

One last thing: [Holding up the black belt] Although I will never become an Olympic gold medal winner like our Master J. Kim, the gold embroidery on the black belt is like the gold medal—symbolic of being a winner. The belt is not just a strip of black cloth. It is a symbol of winning through *perseverance*.

I would like all of you to give a big hand for all those here on the floor today who also *persevered*, and for the families and friends who encouraged and supported them, and for their masters and instructors who guided them to this achievement today. Thank you.

Earning the black belt for me is also symbolic of something else; I persevered and in a way, finally conquered that mountain that has plagued me all these years. Symbolically, it represented reaching the summit of Mt. Damavand.

STEPHANIE SHANLEY'S STORY

Stephanie Shanley recently discovered a memoir writing class and has found it to be a wonderfully cathartic expression for the spirit. She lives in the spectacular Pacific Northwest with her husband Mark and her dog Ferguson.

The Mountain and the Typhoon

By Stephanie Shanley

I F ASKED WHAT WAS DISTINCTIVE ABOUT MY FATHER, I WOULD start with his hands. His mechanic's hands were burnished with bruises, cuts, and scrapes, callouses at the base of every finger, and nails never free of grease. His blue-green eyes could squint in anger or glint with mischief, and, in later years, water with emotion. His voice was warm and rumbly when good tempered, blustery and bellowing like a storm if angry. My father was perfectly flawed and I hero-worshipped him.

For the flaws: A quick temper, pig-headed stubbornness, often an unwillingness to see the perspectives of others. He was NOT a morning person (do not attempt any conversation before the second cup of coffee), and he held an honorary Ph.D. in procrastination. The most notable issue was his short fuse. He was a force to be reckoned with when angry. His tendency toward road rage meant it was not fun to be a passenger in his vehicle—add in the Massachusetts traffic. When I was too small to see out the car window, I sensed that rage by how hard he shifted gears in his red VW Carmen Ghia. Plus, the swearing and gesticulating was a clue.

I did everything in my power to not be the focus of his disappointment or that temper. Two times I failed and got a spanking, first at age six then again at ten. You know when you think your child must be dead, or could have died from something reckless, you're so relieved they're alive now you want to kill them? That was the kind of spanking I got. My mother was so distraught by the neighbors hearing my screaming and crying that she absently rearranged everyone's garbage cans. (It was trash day.)

My parents had a short-lived romance that ended in divorce when I was three, but a relentlessly volatile relationship continued well into my adulthood. She was a deeply troubled woman who relied on alcohol to quiet her demons, but it only fueled the desire to strike out at others before they could hurt her. She was a typhoon of dysfunction and damage, with no mercy if you were in her path.

I don't have any memory of my father living with us. He had visitation every other weekend, alternate holidays, and one month each summer. She made his life as miserable as possible, fueled by her alcoholism, and her weapon of choice was me as the pawn. They kept the local police busy, and his well-paid attorney was on speed-dial.

The time spent with my Dad became my absolute best childhood memories. He provided the only sense of normalcy. The simplest things, like regular meals, reading, a TV show, bedtime, were all welcome routines. Special occasions included a meal at Friendly's (an East Coast chain) where we'd get burgers, fries, and a vanilla shake. When we went to the IHOP it was flavorful, sugary pancakes. I loved his grilled cheese; he made them using that solid brick of Velveeta in a box. You couldn't pay me to touch the stuff now, but then it was the most wonderful comfort food.

My Dad's studio apartment and the quaint neighborhood

both had lots of character and provided refuge. They had the best 4th of July parade and block party. Massachusetts was incredibly patriotic. Perhaps you've heard of the football team the New England Patriots? His furnishings were few but comfortable and practical. He had a futon with mission-style wide wooden arms, plaid cushions of brown, gold, and orange woven wool, pilled with use and many of the tufted buttons missing. When I sat on it, my feet just reached the edge of the cushions, and it doubled as my bed. The one thing that went everywhere he lived was a small shelf he built himself. It was multileveled and held his treasures: The constants were a ceramic sailor with a bag on his back, a bobblehead Charlie Brown, and an Aries ram sculpture.

Stand-out memories: It's 1970, my fifth birthday, and he has built me a cedar hope chest. It's engraved and dated in his handwriting and, best of all, my first puppy is inside. He is a cockapoo named Smoky. Dad took me to "Bambi" and every Disney movie that followed. At the Boston aquarium, I remember the fear and exhilaration of a grated walkway that passed over the enormous shark tank! I remember the planetarium, where you could see the night sky in the middle of the day. It was magical. He loved fishing and taught me to put a worm on the hook, but not before teaching me how to swim first. Perhaps my most favorite weekends were camping trips. It was a wonderful escape—no TV, yummy food, great conversation, a mesmerizing fire, a good book, beautiful scenery, and always quality connecting.

One of the first books I recall him reading to me was *Jonathan Livingston Seagull* by Richard Bach, and I credit him for my love of reading. I loved animals, so he gave me the James Herriot series, which cured me of wanting to be a vet, but fueled my passion for animals, especially dogs. We read all the Peanuts comics together, always watched their holiday shows, and often sent each other Charlie Brown & Snoopy cards. The Harry Potter Series hooked us completely. We later shared an affinity for Calvin and Hobbes. Calvin is an imaginative and mischievous boy with a stuffed tiger that is alive only to him. You would rip your hair out if he was your kid, but it's hilarious to read their adventures. My father loved a rebel; he once got kicked out of church for filling his water pistol with holy water and squirting people during mass.

For a bachelor in the '60s and '70s, he was an incredibly dedicated single dad, and he never missed one of our visitations. Where it often went wrong was returning me home, especially when it was evident that my mother had been drinking. The most vivid memory was when I was four or five years old, and it was clear she was intoxicated. She was baiting him to argue, but he was being calm and civil. He offered to get me ready for bed and asked that she get my PJs for him.

Next thing I know, I'm swept up in his arms, he's holding me tight and we are flying down the stairs and back into his VW. He had started the car, and there was my mother screaming and banging on the passenger window, her adrenaline sobering her to action. My father is yelling "LOCK THAT DOOR!" My stomach is churning, my body is shaking, but I obey my father, and, as my small fingers push the lock down, my mother's eyes lock with mine. She stops banging and screaming and just stares. I cry the whole way to his apartment knowing nothing good could come of this—she would make him pay. Shortly after the police arrive, I am returned to my mother, and many more battles ensue. My father tries until I'm eighteen, but he never wins in court. Yet he never stops fighting for me.

We had our ups and downs over the years, as all family do, but our relationship was solid, so we found our way through conflict and grew closer. On his last visit to Oregon, I took him to all the beautiful sights we have. He especially loved the Oregon coast and Mt. Hood. Whenever I see that majestic sight on clear days, I think, "My father was the mountain, constantly challenged by every element intent to conquer him, but his presence remained solid and standing, and always visible to me, even from great distances."

Epilogue: I last saw my father, Richard, in 2015. I flew to New Hampshire to celebrate our milestone birthdays. He had turned seventy-five on April 12th, and I turned fifty on April 14th. Three days later he received a diagnosis of stage-four lung cancer; they gave him a year and a half. I went back in June to help as he planned for chemo, though he had barely survived radiation therapy. He was determined to continue the battle. It never happened. Even hospice staff was surprised by how quickly things happened. I was with him round the clock, reading both *Harry Potter* and *Jonathan Livingston Seagull*. I held his hand and told him how many people called with regrets, love, and well wishes. I wiped his brow, told him how proud I was to be his daughter, that he was the best father I could have hoped for, how missed he would be, and that I believed he would always be watching over me. My dad was my hero and my mountain. I miss him every day.

ELAYNE SHAPIRO'S STORIES

Elayne Shapiro taught interpersonal, family, organizational, and conflict communication at the University of Portland for twenty-eight years. Before arriving in Portland, she lived in Fargo, North Dakota, for ten years. She received her PhD at the University of Minnesota where she met her husband, Leonard. She and Leonard have three sons.

Fargo, Not the Movie

by Elayne Shapiro

WHEN WE MOVED FROM FARGO, I DID NOT KNOW IF I COULD BE happier anywhere else. A few months before we left, I wrote in a diary, "It's hard to think about leaving Fargo without tears welling and my voice cracking. I am grieving." On my way to take Joseph to Montessori, I looked at the dike of the Red River and thought, "How beautiful." Then I thought, "It's not that Fargo is beautiful; a stranger would see it as flat and dull. But for me, because I know it, its safety, its goodness—to me, it is beautiful."

But that is not how my first year in Fargo began. I remember walking down our street holding Daniel's hand and feeling very, very lonely. I met a woman on the block who was pushing a stroller. I was so happy just to have someone to talk to. She asked me if I was still nursing Daniel, who was two at the time. "No," I replied. She looked at me with disdain, and told me that she was head of the La Leche League of Fargo, and I was doing my child harm. I left that conversation still lonely.

Whenever I mention that I used to live in Fargo, North Dakota, people would ask me, "Oh, did you see the movie

Fargo? I would answer, "Yes," but thought to myself, "Did you notice that only two scenes of that movie were located in Fargo?" What was Fargo really like? Not all the people were like the La Leche lady, but to understand Fargo, one needs a sense of its physicality.

I can characterize Fargo best by those things that stood out to me after I moved to Portland. When I lived in Fargo, I did not notice these things. When I moved to Portland, I walked around in a state of wonder. I live on top of a small hill. If I walk through my neighborhood, I can go up or down. The only way one goes up or down in Fargo is using an escalator or an elevator. Fargo is flat. Fargo is part of the Great Plains. Look out into the horizon and it is flat. Look out at the horizon from my house in Portland, and you can see the West Hills and sometimes Mt. Hood.

When I moved to Portland from Fargo, folks wondered what was hanging out of the hood of my car. At first, I didn't know what they were talking about. I looked. "Oh, the cord for the car heater!" The average temperature in the month of January in Fargo is minus nine degrees Fahrenheit. The lowest temperature ever recorded was minus thirty-eight degrees Fahrenheit on January 10, 1982. We lived in Fargo that winter. For the car to start, the battery heater was needed in January and February for sure, but at times it was needed overnight in other months as well.

When I moved to Portland, I gave away my jacket. I had a jacket that would keep me warm to minus eighty degrees. I remember walking to my car with insulated leggings over my pants, and my royal blue down jacket with the hood pulled up. Without the hood and rim of fur blocking the wind from my face, the bits of razor edged sleet would have cut my exposed skin and I would have ended up with frostbite.

During the winter months, I always had to allow extra time to travel a short distance. Here is a classic winter scene. I wanted to go grocery shopping. I climbed into my winter gear. I dressed one or more children in their winter gear—mittens, hat, snowsuit, and boots. We would get buckled in, and one child would say, "I have to go potty." Alternatively, the child might not say "I have to go potty." Nonetheless, he went potty, and all clothes might need changing. Fargo builds patient people.

In Portland, snow tires are optional, and usually it's people who go to the mountain who use them. We had mountains in Fargo too—mountains of plowed snow on every corner. Studded tires were almost requirements for Fargo's winter weather. I could not see oncoming traffic until I was practically in it, and I had to floor the gas pedal to avoid getting hit. Some of my scariest memories in Fargo were left-handed turns. I was also aware that I could just stand outside and die. Every year blizzards took lives.

Spring in Fargo brought with it "no-see-ums." I learned about these creatures one spring day when two-year-old Daniel came into the house with blood running down his face. No-see-ums are bloodsuckers many times smaller than mosquitoes. When mountains of snow melt, they leave puddles of standing water in which the tiny bugs thrive. Typically, they take a bite the size of their bodies, and hence, the blood which ran down Daniel's face.

Spring also brought flowers, but the range was limited. Potted geraniums and peony shrubs did well. Many people had roses. When I moved to Portland, I marveled that crocuses started pushing up at the end of February. Seeing the yellow candle of skunk cabbage in Tryon Creek Park lit up a whole day. I found the spring colors here dazzling—azaleas and rhododendrons in pink, purple, red, orange, yellow, and magenta. One Fargo flower outgrew its Portland counterpart, however—the simple sunflower. We have a picture of Daniel, Ari, and Joseph perched on a ladder in front of a sunflower growing two feet higher than Joseph, who sat on the top rung of the six-foot-high ladder.

Spring came to Fargo about the end of April. Usually, on spring's official start date, March 21, we had snow on the ground. They used to tell a joke in Fargo. "What are you going to do this summer?" The answer was, "It depends. If it comes on the weekend, we'll go to the lakes." Here is another: "We use a really strong sunblock when we go to the beach with the kids. It's SPF 80: You squeeze the tube, and a sweater comes out." Actually, Fargo brags about a 130-degree temperature range because high temperatures in the summer are common. And with them come the mosquitos and tornados.

Once, when Leonard and I were at a movie, the manager turned on the lights and said there was a tornado sighting in north Fargo. We lived in north Fargo. By the time we got to our car, the sky was green. Leonard ran every stop light to get home. Our roof had a dent in it from a hailstorm some months before. A comedian quipped, "If people didn't have the weather to talk about, nine-tenths of them couldn't start a conversation."

After living in Fargo for ten years, however, I didn't know if I could be happy anywhere else. Clearly, the weather was not the main factor, but perhaps it was a little. Because in such a cold place, you come to depend on people a lot. How we found a network of friends begins the next chapter.

Another Thing I Cannot Control

By Elayne Shapiro

"**M**OM'S JUST WALKING IN THE DOOR," MY HUSBAND SAID. "DO you want to Skype?" My alert system clicked into the "on" position. Our middle child is the only one who would call us around the six o'clock hour for a normal conversation, but he called yesterday, and we never Skype. I deduced it was Michael, our youngest son. I knew that calling nine o'clock Eastern Time meant this was not a Skype call; David and Josh would be asleep, and they are the reasons we Skype. Now the question was, "Is this a good call or a bad call? Professional or personal? Pregnancy?"

It was a bad call.

Michael and Anna just found out that the house, which they bought a year ago, had a leak that needed immediate repair. They could sue the previous owners for non-disclosure, but the stress and cost in lawyers' fees would not balance out the cost for them to fix it—thirty thousand dollars. "Did you ever have anything like this?" Michael asked, his voice cracking? We recounted the story of my walking barefoot on the living room carpet and discovering my toes squishing water at each step. At the time, I responded as I usually do in such situations: "LEONARD!!!"

We consulted with our neighbor, Allen, a contractor. A few years before we had a little fountain spurt forth in the middle of our driveway. We learned that, once upon a time, a spring ran near our house. The spring had changed course and was now running under our house. Allen speculated that the spring was flexing its might once again, and that we should install a French drain to divert it for good. We installed a French drain for ten thousand dollars. It did not solve the problem.

Next, we had our radiant heat checked. We tore up our living room carpet, and the person determined that our radiant heat was the problem. We installed a completely different heating system. And the dollars flew out the window. We replaced carpeting in our entire house; more dollars flew out the window. I hoped Michael felt better. He laughed as I told the story, but I could hear in his voice that he did not feel better. He had more to tell.

"Someone tried to break into our house today." I shut my eyes: all the better to feel the dread which streamed from brain to heart to stomach. "They didn't get in," he choked out. The impulse to pick up my little kid who merely scraped his knee was right there. Michael was really hurting. Protecting one's family, vulnerability, helplessness were the causes for his voice breaking up. But he is bigger than I. And he is three thousand miles away. "We were lucky the windows are double-paned. We have cardboard over the windows," he continued.

My first impulses were all wrong. Ask for more information. Give advice. Offer reassurance. I did not act on my initial impulses; my mediation training kicked in. "This stuff is emotionally tough, Michael."

He asked again, "Has this ever happened to you?"

Why do we ask this question? I think we ask this question because we are flung off balance. For a period of time, we feel marginalized from "normal." Everyone else gets to live their lives as normal people for whom bad things don't happen. We, however, wander among the unlucky, and we want to get back to good fortune, so we ask, "Did this ever happen to you?"

I didn't want to just say 'No, we never had a break-in." I wanted to mitigate his feeling. I wanted to lighten his spirit. "Once, when we lived in Fargo, Michael, we rented out the downstairs basement. It had an apartment. Our tenant seemed to have a lot of friends and visitors. We thought he was a very social guy. And then we found out he was dealing drugs. We asked him to leave. He asked if he could have through the weekend. We said sure. We had to go down to Minneapolis that weekend. When we came back, we found out that he had, indeed, moved out, and he left every window open. It was twenty degrees below zero."

I was glad to hear Michael gasp at the other end of the line. "It could have been worse," I continued. "The guy who owned the house before us had tenants who put a hose in the basement window, turned it on, and left."

"And you bought the house anyway?"

"We did. We loved that house." Our conversation turned to whether or not Michael and Anna would be able to sell their house because public records are kept on break-ins. "Michael, when we drove up to the house on our last visit, the Uber driver said, 'Wow, that is a beautiful house!' You live in a wonderful house in the one neighborhood close to campus deemed desirable; you will be able to sell it!" The temptation to reassure could not be suppressed any longer.

"The police said we should get movement sensitive lights to put outside the window."

"What about a camera?" No response.

"They also suggested a dog," he said.

"What about just a sign that said, 'Beware of Dog' and a motion sensitive tape of a barking dog?" my husband threw in.

"Do you remember the circumstances under which we got our first dog, Brandy?" I asked. Michael did remember how vulnerable we all felt when a marketer grilled Ari and him about who lived at our house, whether we had a watchdog, or an alarm. He remembered that we got Brandy, a used cairn terrier, because Toto had scared the Wicked Witch of the West. And we all laughed together.

I said, "Michael, if there is any way we can support you here, let us know. We can lend you the money; we can fly out while work on the house commences. That's what retired parents are for." He declined our offer.

"Before I forget," Michael added, "David chose the strangest book from preschool library to bring home, the chapter book of *Huckleberry Finn*."

"Why *Huckleberry Finn*?" Leonard asked.

"I'm not sure, why. Maybe because it will take a long time to read?"

We said goodbye. Afterwards, Leonard and I hugged in our own powerlessness.

This morning we had an email from Michael: "Given the circumstances, I was a little alarmed this morning when David came into our room well before his usual wakeup time and said he had found something downstairs he wanted to show me urgently.

"The something was: he had put the Huckleberry Finn book on a chair downstairs and wanted me to read the first chapter."

Every time I woke up in the night, I found myself saying the serenity prayer over and over again. But as frequently happens, I made a slight verbal shift. "Grant me the serenity to accept the things I cannot control. The courage to control the things I can. And the wisdom to know the difference." This is not something I can control. Let it go.

KAREN STEPHENS'S STORY

Karen Stephens holds a master's degree in education and has worked as a teacher for more than twenty years. She is also an artist and loves to travel. This will be her first published work, and she has plans to publish her memoir. She lives in Lake Oswego, Oregon, with her beloved cat, Baby, and Domingo, her partner of seventeen years.

Treasures of the Heart

By Karen Stephens

"More valuable than treasures in a storehouse are
the treasure of the body, and the treasures of the
heart are the most valuable of all."

Nichiron Daishonin

M Y FIRST INTRODUCTION TO THE COMPLEXITIES OF
grandmotherhood came from an older female friend
who had many grandbabies via her two sons and daughter.
It seemed to me every conversation with her was dominated
by news about at least one grandbaby and what he or she was
up to, and, of course, how incredibly adorable each one was.
Grandchildren were the be-all and end-all in this friend's
world. Whenever we saw one another, which was frequent, I
would sit and listen with fascination as she glowingly spoke of
her grandbabies. Little did I know that she was preparing me
for the future. I am eternally grateful to her.

It never occurred to me that I, too, would one day be a
grandmother. As much as I desired such a position, I knew
the likelihood was slim to none. My son Hayden, a handsome,

athletic, intelligent man, had been diagnosed with a severe mental illness at the age of seventeen. His illness prevents him from maintaining romantic relationships, and thus, potential grandbabies. Of course, there would always be the concern that his children would also suffer from mental illness. So, I suppose all is as it should be.

Nevertheless, six years ago, my partner's son introduced his baby boy to us. It was a lovely surprise to be gifted with baby Lincoln. I recall the first time we met. Lincoln was carried into my home in a baby chair carrier—a tiny little guy with curly brown hair, a sweet round face, and huge blue eyes. He was quiet and attentive. His little face and those big blue eyes watched every move I made. He was in a strange environment, clearly frightened of these two big people hovering around him. My heart went out to him. I made it my mission to make him feel safe.

So, even though my first instinct was to sweep him up to cuddle, I approached him carefully, softly, introducing myself, behaving as though he was a fellow adult rather than cooing or using baby talk. The more I spoke, the more he relaxed. His little face followed mine with curiosity until his tension faded and he started talking back to me. A baby's first voice must be one of the most wondrous, delightful sounds known to humankind. When he blessed me with a big smile, I felt like I had just won the Publishers Clearing House Sweepstakes. Lincoln's magic lay in his trusting, pure soul. The bond created with Lincoln revived my buried tenderness. That tenderness had been kept away in my heart, not to be exposed in order protect myself from being hurt. This child had no agenda. He did not judge my appearance, nor did he care how much I weighed, my career, how much money I made, or what car I drove. He loved and loves me because I am me. Glorious!

Over the years, as Grandma Karen and little Lincoln have created an endearing relationship, he refers to me as his favorite grandma. Such a compliment, as he has two other grandmas, one who lives with his dad and is raising him and also his mother's mother, whom he sees every weekend. I spend one day a week with Lincoln. Every week I go out of my way to come up with new eclectic adventures for us.

He has introduced me to Chuck E. Cheese, insisting I play all the games with him. To the Oregon Museum of Science and Industry (OMSI), where we explore the children's section, both of us on the floor constructing structures with wooden blocks. To the Portland Children's Museum, where we pretend we are grocery shopping or play puppeteers for one another. To Pump It Up, where little ones play on inflated play structures. To Sky High, the clever indoor trampoline emporium. To various arcades, which cost a small fortune. We have also visited swimming pools, indoor and outdoor, where I taught him to swim. Having his little arms around my neck, laughing with glee or singing his favorite songs is such a wonderful thing. Knowing he trusts me to not drown us is a testament to how much faith he has in his Grandma Karen. That creates in me a feeling of powerful importance, right up there with Wonder Woman.

My favorite adventure with Lincoln, when the weather allows, is exploring some of the many amazing Portland Parks. Tryon Park State Park, close by my home, is one we frequent. Educating Lincoln to the wonders of nature is important to me because nature was instrumental in soothing me during childhood. Friends I have known have explained to me that the out of doors is their religion. They have told me that they feel the presence of God while being alone hiking or fishing. I think I understand their sentiments.

As a single mother, raising my son alone all those years, nature was our go-to place. Hayden loved the out of doors, even going so far as to skip school to wander around by the river with our German shepherd dog, BJ. We hiked, cross-country skied, swam in the rivers, lakes, and ocean. Nature bonded us, it was free, and it gave us exercise, wonderful smells, sites, access to wildlife. Nature tended to our souls. To this day, Hayden takes long walks daily to be close to nature. It is in is bones. I so want to give Lincoln the same gift I gave my son—a love of nature. A safe place to find solace. One of the most precious resources we possess.

During our first nature walk I pointed out ferns, moss, plants and birds. Lincoln was easily engaged, learning the names of each plant, tree, and bird I identified. It was a game we played together as we walked along the trails. Each new living thing captivated him, motivating him to want to learn more, see more, ask more questions. Seeing him enjoying himself was my reward. I so wanted him fall in love with nature, to see how magical it is, to be transformed by its wonders, to help him experience the peace and calming effects it bestows. Now, whenever I see his little face brighten, asking about future visits to nature, it warms my heart. As far as I know, I am the only adult who takes Lincoln on nature walks. It is my hope I will leave a legacy for my sweet grandson to pass on to his children.

Sometimes I ponder those things I've introduced to him. I am certain he is aware of how I love him unconditionally. He knows he can act as silly as he likes without my shaming him. He knows laughter is the best medicine. He knows learning can be enjoyable. He knows Grandma Karen will not yell at him when he misbehaves. He knows he is always forgiven. He knows I am a constant in his life and will never abandon him. Important stuff for a little man.

On his behalf, Lincoln has taught me:

1. When I tell you to "watch" while I am doing something important, like jumping on a trampoline or swinging on the monkey bars, it is vital that you do not miss one second. Checking messages on your phone or looking at another child when told to "watch" is downright devastating. A sure sign you do not love me.

2. Force yourself to forgo any sense of dignity while playing

with me. Please be willing to act silly, chase me in front of other grownups, laugh and giggle when we play. After all, this is a great opportunity to have a second childhood. (In my case, I never had my first one, being the eldest child in my family.) Throw all restraints to the wind. When other adults look at you like you're nuts, ignore them. They simply have no clue as to what they are missing.

3. Get off the couch and dance with me. Don't just watch—participate. Show enthusiasm while singing with me (even if you are off-key). Let it all hang out. Act like you are a kid while we are playing board games.

4. Do not discipline me like you were disciplined. Fear and shame are outdated. Spanking is primitive torture.

5. Listen to me when I talk to you. No watching TV, talking on the phone, or reading a book when I need your attention.

6. Treat me with the respect you would a fellow adult. And no, children are no longer to be seen and not heard. Somebody got that all mixed up. It is rather "Children are precious and have much wisdom for adults," so listen to me, spend time with me. I am your gift.

7. No matter what, Grandma, know I love and adore you. My opinion of you is far more important than that of other adults. They don't see what a goddess you truly are.

To say Lincoln has made a huge impact in my life would be an understatement. If only I could, like Auntie Mame, indulge Lincoln in the finer things in life—introduce him to classical music or a children's theater, travel to exotic places, treat him to special, expensive, learning camps, lavish him with all the opportunities of wealthy children so he will be successful in his manhood. A great dream. What I do have for Lincoln however, are the treasures of the heart. Treasures of the heart beyond treasures of the body, or treasures of the storehouse. Treasures of the heart, the most important treasure in life. Everything else pales in comparison.

CHRISTOPHE
STICKEL'S STORIES

Christophe Stickel dropped out of a Ph.D. program in English literature at the University of Washington to become a chef apprentice at the Olympic Hotel in Seattle. Three years later, he worked in luxury hotels in Switzerland and England. Christophe eventually wound up in San Francisco, where for fourteen years he was the executive chef of the San Francisco Golf Club. He left the cooking business to become a leading dealer in signed books and autographs. He now lives in Lake Oswego, Oregon, with his wife, Susan Scott, and their two Yorkshire terriers. He is currently working on a culinary mystery that takes place in St. Moritz, Switzerland.

What I've Learned in My Memoir Class

By Christophe Stickel

FOR THE LAST YEAR, I'VE BEEN TAKING A WEEKLY TWO-HOUR memoir writing class at the Lake Oswego Adult Community Center. Each week, most students write, then read, a three-page story. Every six or seven weeks we start a new session, which means we often get new students along with the veterans. Last week a new student said she wasn't sure if this were the right class for her because she wants to learn how to write. As she read a blog entry she wrote about her son attending an exclusive academy, this student proved she could write.

I'm confident that if this woman stays with the course and writes every week, she will become a much better writer, even though this is not a how-to writing class. I noticed a definite improvement in all the writing of those students who stayed for a year or more. Those students learned tools to help them excel in writing. I too discovered writing tools that make me a better writer. Here are the ones obvious to me.

Writing tool number one: Listen and learn from your class-mates. My fellow students have inspired and instructed me. On my second class I was blown away by a student's essay about buying a bottle of rare olive oil at a gourmet store. Such a topic shouldn't be funny or clever. Well, this story was. The writer expertly weaved an event in the past with droll comments and reflections in the present. After listening to this story, I learned writing had no hard and fast rules. You don't have to tell a story chronologically. This student's account inspired me to write outside the box. My wife is also in my class. Susan is the funniest person I know. Every day she makes me laugh. She is also a gifted writer. Not many writers have their first book published in hardcover by a major New York publisher. This talent to be funny also shows up in her stories, no matter what the subject. I now try whenever possible to include humor in my stories. One more reason why I love my wife.

Writing tool number two: A writing class makes you accountable. Last summer, there were no classes for eight weeks. I planned to write a piece every week. Guess how many stories I had when class resumed in the fall? You guessed it— One measly essay. I didn't have the discipline to write on my own. I needed the impetus of this class.

Writing Tool Number Three: Try to write every day. We all lead busy lives, so it's tough to take time to think, write, and rewrite a 1,200-word essay every week. Nothing will improve your craft more than just writing. Last November I wrote a 50,000-word novel. Only seventeen percent of those who signed up at NaNoWriMo.com finished their books.

Every day in November I wrote 1,667 words. The result was transformational for me. I can spend up to ten hours preparing and writing a three-page essay. I'm never happy with what I write, so I keep rewriting ad nauseam. The NaNoWriMo advisers urged us this time to avoid editing but just to write. Edit next year, the advisers said. Speedy writing every day was liberating. I am now a better writer just because of this experience. My NaNoWriMo writing buddy Dana also shared the same experience.

Writing tool number four: Edit your work. I know only one writer who can sit down for one hour and write what appears to be a word-perfect three-page essay. Unless you're like this writer, don't turn in your unedited first draft. My first draft is a starting place and rarely resembles my final work. Usually I spend more time editing than writing. For example, I wrote the first draft of this essay in one-and-a-half hours. Editing and rewriting took three times as long, an additional four-and-a-half hours. Before I show my writing to the public, I first read it out loud to myself and then to my wife. I then ask myself this final question: Will my reader be better off after reading my writing? I then make final adjustments, making sure I leave my reader with a gift, such as a new idea, a recommendation, or something funny or heartwarming.

Writing tool number five: Less is more. If you asked successful writers to list their favorite writing books, *The Elements of Style* by Will Strunk and E. B. White would be on their list. It's a small book that comprises everything you need to know to excel in writing. The book consists of rules of usage and composition, but no rule is more important than this one: Omit needless words. Stephen King, in his best-selling book, *On Writing. A Memoir on the Craft*, said the best advice he ever received was to eliminate ten percent of the words from his first draft.

Writing tool number six: Read to write better. Occasionally in my classes, Louise, my instructor, as well as other students, recommend books on writing, including those already mentioned, as well as Anne Lamott's *Bird by Bird*. I would add two other books. The first is *On Writing Well* by William Zinsser. There's a reason why more than a million people bought this book. The second book is *Fearless Writing: How to Create Boldly and Write with Confidence* by William Kenower. I heard him speak last year at the Willamette Writer's monthly meeting. His message is that you need to write honestly and fearlessly. Don't write for others. Please yourself and have fun in the process. This book helped me when I began my novel.

Besides books on writing I now seek out good writing no matter where I find it. Returning recently from the Oregon coast, my wife and I stopped at the Sunset Rest Area on U.S. Highway 26. My wife couldn't figure out why I had my notebook open in front of a traveler information board describing the Tillamook Burn, a catastrophic forest fire. Here is part of what I copied: "On August 14, 1933, a bone-dry wind **caught** sparks from a logging operation. In 10 days, the fire **spread** over 40,000 acres. Then, **pushed** by east winds, it **exploded**, scorching another 200,000 acres. Finally, the wind **died**, and rain **soaked** the land." Strong verbs like "caught," "pushed," "spread," "exploded," "died" and "soaked" create a powerful image. Because of his or her bold, clear writing in the active voice, this anonymous author must have mastered *The Elements of Style*.

These are just six tools that I've learned in my memoir class. If you want more writing tools, I recommend *Writing Tools. Fifty Essential Strategies for Every Writer* by Roy Peter Clarke. For me, for now, six tools are plenty, and I hope they will help the new student. Welcome to our class.

Fake Friends

OR HOW MUCH WILL I HAVE TO
PAY FOR YOU TO BE MY FRIEND?

By Christophe Stickel

I DON'T HAVE A LOT OF FRIENDS, SO I FOLLOWED THE ADVICE OF that wise guy, Gordon Kekko, in the movie *Wall Street*: If you need a friend, get a dog.

I first met Gatsby nine years ago at the home of a dog breeder in Sacramento, California. I was in search of the perfect puppy. Six animated pint-sized five-week-old Yorkshire terrier puppies, five boys and one girl, performed somersaults and other acrobatics on Betty's shag carpet. As I lay flat on my belly, trying with my Nikon to capture photos of the puppies, one little boy distracted me. This puppy would not leave me alone. He kept running up to me to plant kisses on my cheek. I gently pushed him away, but he persisted. The breeder saw an opportunity for a sale when she announced, "Ah, I see this puppy has already bonded with you." Moments later, I left a deposit with Betty and agreed to return in three weeks to pick up my new friend.

Apart from Gatsby, my wife Susan is my one constant friend. This May, we will celebrate our thirty-second anniversary. Not once have I ever regretted marrying her. We have both grown, matured, learned and been nourished from our long, loving relationship. There's one problem, however. Susan is a friend magnet. I am not. When we moved to Oregon a year and a half ago, it only took Susan a week to make a friend. She attended a writing class, and before she even entered the room, a woman greeted her like an old friend and asked her out to lunch. Susan now has more friends than I can count. Since we've been in Oregon, she's had dozens of luncheon dates with friends. I'm still waiting for a luncheon buddy.

Susan is my opposite. She is funny, warm, witty, flamboyant, and most important, an extrovert. I, on the other hand, am shy, tongue-tied, and spend most of my time alone. I'm your typical introvert. Although I long for friends, I have very few, but I do have many fake friends. Fake friends are people who are paid in some way to like you. Your waiter may act like your best friend, but if don't pay your bill or tip him poorly, all warmth and humanity vanish.

Many years ago, I realized I had a talent for making fake friends. Susan and I had spent a week at the Heritage House, a luxury retreat in Mendocino, California. At that time, all food was included with lodging, and we were assigned one waitress for the week. The first night our waitress, Emily, served us, she was aloof and even haughty. Instead of enjoying the spectacular ocean view from the Same Time Next Year suite, Susan and I bitched about the poor service.

The next day our waitress remained cold but every time she came to our table I asked her a question. Where did she live? How long had she worked at the Heritage House? Was she married? How many children did she have? Could she show me pictures of her children? I was friendly, and I tipped well. Over the course of the week, Emily became more welcoming and more attentive to our needs. When we now sat down at her station, she gave each of us a big smile and immediately brought us our desired beverage without our having to ask. When we left, she appeared genuinely sorry to see us go.

Since then, as a fake extrovert I have made hundreds of fake friends similar to Emily. Let me take you through a typical day in the pursuit of fake friends in Lake Oswego, Oregon. At 5:45 a.m., I enter Starcycle, Lake Oswego's spinning studio. The 6:00 a.m. class consists of about twenty dedicated athletes. I know all their names; some of them even know mine. I always sit way in the corner. The man next to me is Cort, a handsome, tall man with sculpted biceps who looks like a Greek god. On my first day of class, I asked him what he did for a living. He said he was a banker. "Which bank?" I asked. "Umpqua," he replied.

Over the months, I asked him many questions while we waited for the class to begin, but it took him two-and-a-half months before he spoke to me first. He asked me, "How are you?" I was thrilled. Following this triumph, I did a Google search using the keywords "Cort" and "Umpqua bank." I learned the man who sweats next to me every weekday morning in his designer blue sleeveless shirt is the CEO of Umpqua bank and his annual salary is $1,586,647. No wonder he ignores me. Lately, however, he seems to be a little more friendly. I won't stop talking to him until he becomes my fake friend, just like Emily, the Mendocino waitress.

When I leave Starcycle, I walk next door to Imagine Yoga where I attend the 7:00 a.m. yoga class. Susanna is my yoga teacher and one of my dearest fake friends. She is from Mexico and the morning after Trump was elected, she fought back her tears throughout our class. She wears multicolored yoga pants and reads us poetry; she reminds us to breathe and leads us through a series of postures while she laughs and makes jokes, many of which I don't understand because of her Mexican accent, but I laugh anyway because that's what fake friends do.

After class, I then go to the nearby Safeway, where I talk

at length with Janet, the gay produce manager who tells me about how her mother cured her diabetes by drinking green juices. When I check out my purchases, I have a conversation with Johnny, who is a stand-up comic and writes sci-fi novels. If I have time, I will visit the new Whole Foods 365 supermarket. I'll buy a fresh apple and beet juice from Alex at the Canteen Juice Bar. Alex is on a juice fast, and he tells me how much weight he has lost. I check out the produce department to get gardening tips from Amber, who grows apple trees and is a vegan, but lately, she has some health issues. If I'm lucky, I'll hear a joke from James, the head cashier, who is famous for his smile and his hats. The day before Thanksgiving, he wore a rooster hat. He let me take his picture, and it's one of the photos that I treasure and look at when I feel sad.

I return home where I do chores, write, work on my novel, read, spend time with Susan or walk around the house or backyard while Gatsby follows my every move from the moment I enter the house. I am supremely grateful that I have a true friend for life, and the initial cost was only 2,200 dollars plus 176 dollars in California sales tax. The Beatles were wrong. Money *can* buy you love.

A Portlandia St. Patrick's Day

Christophe Stickel

M Y WIFE, SUSAN, AND I, ALONG WITH OUR FRIEND, DANA, ARE taking a twelve-week class based on Julia Cameron's *The Artist Way*. The course requires that once a week you go on a solo artist date. You set aside about two hours to nurture your "creative consciousness." You could visit an art gallery, paint a picture, stroll through a botanical garden or do any activity you define as art. For my artist date for Saturday, March 17, I had planned to attend a lecture on growing roses, but when I realized that this was St. Patrick's day, I came up with a different plan and a goal. Portland has a reputation for being weird, so I decided to take a bus from Lake Oswego into Portland and then to find and photograph weird people celebrating St. Patrick's Day.

Just before noon, I got off the bus near Burnside Avenue in Portland. Where was everybody? The whole city seemed deserted. Then I discovered where the inhabitants were. They were all at Voodoo Doughnut, the perfect place to begin my quest for weirdness. Voodoo Doughnut is an international tourist destination. The company has its own record label and hosts midnight doughnut-eating contests. Television programs, including the *Tonight Show, Grimm, Leverage,* and of course *Portlandia* have all featured Voodoo Doughnut. More than two hundred people waited patiently in line to choose from more than a hundred kinds of doughnuts, many of which are made with unusual ingredients such as Cap'n Crunch, grape Tang, M&M's, Oreo cookies, marshmallows, and bacon. If you come, bring cash, and prepare to wait. I recommend the Voodoo Doll doughnut.

Voodoo Doughnut, where hundreds of people gather twenty-four seven to eat bizarre food, was a great place to start, but no one looked weird or different. They looked like hungry tourists. I was about to move on when I noticed a humongous green figure at the front of the line. At first, I thought the man was an actor hired by Voodoo to promote the store. No. This man was on a mission to get doughnuts.

Apart from his Irish attire, this jolly green giant looked like a Viking warrior straight out of a Netflix television series. The man was over six feet tall, weighed well over three hundred pounds and had a round pleasant face with a droopy mustache and an unkempt beard. He wore a green-trimmed black bowler hat and a bright green gold-button vest. His broad black belt held up a knee-high woolen kilt. Because he wore no socks, his leather sandals showed off his polished green toenails.

I could never have dreamt of a better subject, but there was a problem. He was half-way through the front door, therefore much of his body was hidden. I snapped a photo of him, but it wasn't good enough. I left and followed the crowd to the Portland Saturday Market, the largest outdoor craft market in the entire country.

There were hundreds of vendors selling food, clothes and craft items. One man in a black tuxedo sold balloon animals. Another vendor drew portraits. Another dealer sold vintage teacups suspended from the ceiling. I saw hundreds of people; some of them wore green in honor of St. Patrick's day; others proudly carried the distinctive pink Voodoo doughnut box. Most of them were ordinary people enjoying the mild weather. Last year's St. Patrick's Day was bitterly cold and it rained all day.

Only a few people met my strict requirements that they must look different and in some way had to be celebrating St. Patrick's day. After fifteen minutes in the market I saw an elegant middle-aged black woman wearing a shamrock scarf and a green hat with a large button that read "Drunk 4." She smiled brightly as she looked at some jewelry. A few minutes later I saw a middle-aged woman with a matching shamrock scarf. She laughed as she bought a cup of fresh melon wedges. I photographed each of them separately, but I wanted them together. In time I got my chance. The couple posed for a woman holding at arm's length an iPhone. As the woman with the iPhone took her photo, I moved to the left of her and got the perfect portrait. None of the women even noticed I was there.

I liked the photo of the couple, but I needed more. I got lucky. The Viking had left Voodoo Doughnut and was now in the market. I still couldn't get a good photo of him because either he only showed me his backside or his six family members kept him partially hidden. Thirty minutes later I spied the Viking standing away from his entourage, and I took the shot. After I lowered my camera, I saw him looking straight at me. I smiled and waved back at him. I was nervous. He didn't smile or show any emotion, but I swear I saw a twinkle in his eyes.

The lunch crowd thinned out, so I had fewer opportunities to photograph. As I was about to leave, a group of exuberant costumed men and women jumped out of a van and scampered toward a food truck. I photographed some of their antics, including one man who proved you could still be a flasher while being fully clothed.

One of the rules of street photography is that you don't let people know you are taking their photos. If they know, then they don't act naturally. I couldn't hide my bulky Nikon professional camera, but I thought I could remain invisible because my telephoto lens allowed me to be far away from my subject.

Taking clandestine photos, however, isn't necessary or even possible for the Portland area. People here love to have their photographs taken, so when this gang of St. Patrick's day holiday makers saw me taking photos, they went out of their way to ham it up in front of my camera. These pranksters called attention to themselves in the best possible way. When I took their photographs, I felt like I was taking pictures of friends and not strangers.

It now rained, so I headed back to my bus stop. A few blocks before my destination, I saw two women in a parking lot dressed in full-length white dresses. One woman had her back to me, but I had to take their photo because one of the women looked like a goat. Long white decorated horns protruded from the sides of her head. Apparently, the women noticed me taking their picture from fifty feet away because they turned around to face me. They laughed, waved their hands and greeted me with thousand-watt smiles. Their playful actions filled with good cheer and joy reminded me of how much I appreciate the warm, fun-loving people of Portlandia, I mean Portland, and how wonderful and satisfying weirdness can be. Erin go Bragh!

LILLIAN "LILY"
STONE'S STORIES

Lillian "Lily" Stone was born in Sioux City, Iowa, in 1950 and is a resident of Southwest Portland. She received her associate's degree in not-for-profit management from Lewis & Clark College. She has worked in the legal community for more than thirty years as a legal secretary, paralegal, office manager, and trial assistant. She loves dogs, cats, and other living creatures, including those growing in her garden. She enjoys writing and also remodeling her 1942 bungalow. She describes herself as a "professional thrifter" and sells antiques and collectibles on eBay.

Facing My Fears

By Lily Stone

M Y "TO DO" LIST USED TO INCLUDE FACING, ERASING, REMOVING, eradicating, and eliminating my top three fears: the fear of flying, the fear of heights and the fear of water. I conquered my fear of flying almost thirty years ago; my fear of heights about twenty-one years ago; and my fear of water, which included the fears of drowning and being unable to swim in an emergency, almost eight years ago. I actually learned how to swim at the age of fifty-nine.

Before I pat myself on the back—and you all stand up and cheer me—I must confess that I am still living with three of my worst fears, although I have camouflaged them expertly. They each wear a disguise, slink around me wherever I go, and many times cause me a great deal of stress and trepidation. Their proper names are confrontation, anger, and just saying no.

It has been a long and rough journey, but it's about time I break up with "Yes" and begin going steady with "No." I have been practicing all week on different individuals, with some success. "I don't think you ever said no—to anyone," said one of my relatives. "Are you sure?" That question is the best way to ensure that I will change my mind and say yes because I get embarrassed.

Instead, I immediately responded, "I have to answer NO at this time. I can't come to the party. I'll let you know if something opens up, okay?" Obviously, I need to continue "Yes Therapy," for it's still number one on my fear list. However, being aware of this problem is the first step. Implementing the "NO" rule reaffirms my desire to change myself.

Anger has been my go-to fear whenever I am standing close to anyone with an anger problem. If an angry man is yelling at a grocery clerk, I just turn around, taking my food stuffs with me, and go to another line—far away from the angry person. No matter how hard I avoid anger, it crawls back into my life when I least expect it. I have assisted a battered wife while her angry husband was belittling her in words and actions in my office parking lot. I have also gone to the aid of an elderly woman who was being berated and humiliated by her caregiver/daughter.

Two weeks ago, I intervened when an angry mother yelled at and began to spank her daughter in public for misbehaving in a grocery store aisle. I even confront people who are striking their animal at the dog park. "Please leave," I demanded of one angry pet-owner. "No one here wants to see you strike that beautiful animal. If you can't control yourself, just leave." I think we all see behavior that warrants some form of intervention. Anger is a giant trigger for me personally.

I received some great advice from my twenty-seven-year-old nephew, Dion, regarding my third fear—that of confrontation. "Dion, I have a question for you," I said to him. "If someone you are friends with at water aerobics starts a conversation by stating, 'My husband told me the funniest nigger joke this morning,' what should I say to her?" I explained to Dion that it wasn't fear of losing the friendship that I worried about, but the actual confrontation, future anger, shaming and being considered a pariah by her and her friends. Without the slightest hesitation, Dion said, "You have a nephew, my half-brother, who is African-American. Would Daksha enjoy this joke if she told it to him? Put her to the test. Start by saying, 'My African-American nephew would not appreciate this joke.'"

His response was so simple and so honest that I realized I was worrying about something I could completely change about myself. I could say those words with conviction. I realized that I'd been so shocked by this woman's use of the "N" word that all my common sense went out the window. Telling the truth is always the answer, but I also realized that I tend to answer someone's question immediately, without giving the question more thought.

I posed the same question to my forty-year-old daughter, Heather, one night, and she gave me a completely different response. "No, no, no, no way, not going there," she said. She chuckled and told me she would walk away from the woman, still saying no and still chuckling. "She doesn't deserve to learn that you have an African-American nephew."

She then pointed to me and said, "Mom, you can kill three of your fears with one stone. By saying "NO," you are practicing the art of saying "NO." By walking away, you are avoiding a confrontation. A confrontation may end in anger and you have eliminated that possibility. Finally, you are taking the power away from the situation and the woman and placing it firmly into your own hands. I guess you are now one step closer to being fearless."

Being Watched

By Lily Stone

OCTOBER 31, 1967

I WAS NEARLY SEVENTEEN YEARS OLD AND A SENIOR AT NORTH Catholic High School. The following June I would graduate. But there would be no summer vacation for me. On July 1, I would begin a six-month stint at Portland Secretarial School. I would learn everything necessary to obtain a full-time legal secretarial position in a law firm. My parents insisted that I graduate from the school's one-year program after just six months because the school charged eighty dollars per month in tuition. They could come up with four-hundred eighty dollars for the tuition and twenty dollars for the books.

My senior year was no different from the previous three years for me. I could not sign up for sports, clubs, the school newspaper, or any extracurricular activities. "To and from school, Lillian, no stops for any reason," my parents would say to me every Monday morning. "Understand?"

"Yes," I'd reply each time. "To and from school and no stops whatsoever."

Every other Friday I would buy 45 rpm records with hits like "Brown-Eyed Girl" by Van Morrison, "The Letter" by the Box Tops, "To Love Somebody" by the Bee Gees, and "Light My Fire" by Jim Morrison. The record shop was two doors down from the high school, and it was impossible to not stop and learn the top rock-and-roll hits for the month. The 45s were on sale every Friday, two for ninety-nine cents. What a deal! I couldn't imagine what life would be like without music.

One thing did change during my senior year. My oldest sister, Maxine, graduated and I no longer had to walk to and from school with her. She held down a part-time job at the U.S. Post Office, shuffling letters and packages in the back office. I was now free to walk home alone, take my time to browse the outside windows of the neighborhood stores. I always stopped at the pet store, my favorite shop, and it was next to the record store. The puppies were so friendly and even the kittens acknowledged my presence. At the back of the store was a new arrival: a woolly monkey. I was told it was six months old and came from the jungles of South America. It was a medium-to large-sized primate with a strong prehensile tail. "A prehensile tail," I thought. "I will look that up when I get home." The woolly monkey gets its name from its soft, thick, curled fur, which ranges in color from brown to black to gray, depending on the species. Woolly monkeys have relatively stocky bodies, with powerful shoulders and hips.

I called this ape "handsome" for obvious reasons. He poked his fingers through the bars of his cage and touched my hand. I was not afraid, and, in fact, I spoke to him for some time alone. I asked the owner of the pet store if I could help her with his grooming, cleaning his cage, feeding, etc. She said she couldn't pay me much, but I insisted that I could only work weekdays from 2:30 to 4:30. "Is that ok with you?" I queried. "I would be a volunteer and you would not have to pay me. I will add this job to my resume and that is enough for me." She agreed and I stayed that Friday afternoon until almost five o'clock.

When I got home, I squirreled away my two 45 rpm records and sought out the encyclopedia to research the woolly monkey. I knew that I could only be Handsome's friend, not a potential adoptive owner. Puppies and kittens were one thing, but a primate was another. My father had already had "the talk" with me about trying to adopt a de-skunked skunk from the Oregon Humane Society more than a year ago. "What's wild must always stay wild," he'd said. "A wild animal deserves to remain wild in almost all cases. Do you agree, Lillian?"

"Yes, yes I do agree," I'd responded. Little did he know that every day after school I would spend two hours at the pet store, assisting the owner with tropical fish, dogs, cats, other various pets, and a woolly monkey.

I learned valuable lessons that year, but the most significant to me was taking care of the pet-store occupants. I was used to being constantly watched and over-protected for too long by my parents. One day, though, I would be free and able to do what I wanted, without fear of being found out, caught, or teased. "Handsome" would never be really "free" ever again. Once he was caught, he lost all hope of freedom. Yes, his adoptive parents would watch him, just like I was watched and cared for; but I have to believe that we all need some watching, a great deal of loving and lots of respect. My wish for him was to be cared for by a loving person or persons who truly respected him as he was—a wild animal.

RONALD TALNEY'S
STORIES

Ronald Talney is a retired lawyer, a poet, and writer who has published five volumes of poetry, two novels, a memoir, and numerous individual poems and personal essays. He writes a monthly column, "My World," in the *Lake Oswego Review*. He and his wife, Linnette, live in Lake Oswego, Oregon.

The Still Creek Bridge:
An Anniversary Essay

By Ronald Talney

FROM THIS NARROW, ONE LANE, WOODEN BRIDGE WE CAN SURVEY Still Creek from two perspectives, one to the south where in spring the waters cascade down off Mt. Hood, the other to the north where the creek will eventually merge with the Zig Zag River another mile or two down-stream, just below Rhododendron. The view to the south is green and softer at this time of year, late August, the creek now shallow and gentle. Soon salmon will return, struggling up and up from the sea in their long quest for home. They will batter themselves across the rocks that jut from just beneath the surface of the stream, as they throw themselves from one eddy to another, over one barrier, then another, their blackened bodies barely still alive.

We come here to the foothills of the Cascades often, and in every season, to see again the best evidence of who we are: Laurel Canyon, Flag Mountain, the marks left of wagons and people heading west on the Barlow Trail. But especially at this time in late August, as it is where we have come to acknowledge our own time together. Soon it will be fall again. And then winter.

There is a morning chill in the air already. Set against the backdrop of tall firs and pine, the deciduous trees that dip their lower branches over the creek are beginning to shed their leaves into the swirling waters. The vine maples are turning, first a faint yellow and then deepening finally to a flaming orange and red. Together we stand, first on one side of the bridge, looking to the north, and then on the other, looking south. We never vary from this ritual. We never cease to marvel, both at the view and at the fact that we are still here, together, still holding this vision in our hearts of a place on this earth where we are totally at peace. Where the marriage of what the eye sees is complete and whole.

Soon, when the snow falls, and the banks of the creek fill with white and the snow piles onto the rocks and the railings of the bridge, we will again walk down this narrow road, hand in hand. We will again check the spot where only last summer we saw the ghostly white stems of Indian pipe, their now black and dying stalks still visible, rising up out of the drifts. We might see wood ducks swimming against the current, their brilliant colors flashing in the sun. Then again, like today, we will be alone here, just the two of us, alone with the murmur of the creek, the gentle swirling of water as it slides beneath us., and the sweet silence of old growth.

A Dance of Wind

By Ronald Talney

OUR SPECIAL BENCH SITS, NO MATTER THE SEASON OR THE weather, just off the asphalt path that winds down through the forested hills of Mountain Park, bordering Spring Creek. Over time, its wood planks have weathered to a silvery brown, lighter in color and shinier than its original cedar finish. The small brass plaque remains as it was, however.

> TO THE MEMORY OF
> ALLISON ELAINE TALNEY
> 1965-1988
> "I WILL SPEAK TO YOU
> NOT WITH WORDS BUT WITH MOVEMENTS
> A DANCE OF WIND."

This bench and its plaque were placed here soon after Linnette and I moved to Mountain Park, when we first walked this path and felt movement in the surrounding fir trees, their limbs gently swaying in the breeze, and the leaves of maple trees drifting down in their slow dance around our feet. It was fall, and it seemed such a mysterious and unseen force. We stopped to rest and quickly felt our daughter's presence. It was here on this curve of path we asked permission to place this bench in her memory.

It is located about halfway downhill, between where we live and the local shopping center. Folks coming up from the New Seasons Market, along the creek and through the woods, carrying their heavy bags of groceries can stop here and rest, as we often do. From time to time, as I walk down the path and past the bench, an elderly man or woman will be sitting there holding sacks of groceries and enjoying a few moments of respite. He or she will nod and smile, seemingly grateful for this small oasis but unaware of what connection I might have, if any, to the bench.

We too have rested here many times. Her death is far behind us now, but with us always in ways the world will never see. Our lives are strangely normal. We live each day in her absence, caught in this space between belief and disbelief. Knowing she is gone but never far.

The last time we saw Allison alive, we were taking her to the airport, a task we had performed so many times before. She was returning to New York to resume her work for an international airline as a flight attendant, following a period of mild illness that had kept her grounded and at home. We dropped her off at Portland International Airport as usual. We said our goodbyes as usual. None of us could have anticipated the tragedy that would soon occur, the events beyond our control. We did not know our lives were about to be changed forever. I have often wondered how it would have been different if we had known. I would have held her and not let go. Like any father would, I would not have let her go. But I did. And she was gone.

And now it is this bench that remains. This bench that has become such a symbol of our new life. This is our quiet place where the breezes at all times of the year move the limbs of the evergreen trees, making them sway to her unseen presence, where maple leaves in the fall still drift down and cover the ground at our feet. Where birds in springtime build their nests, and where in summer squirrels gather nuts, preparing for winter's blast. Here too we can sit, husband and wife, father and mother, still together, still watching the seasons change, time move on and on in its own slow way. A resting place. A place where stillness lives between the past and the future.

"I will speak to you, not with words but
with movement, a dance of wind."

If only I had known. If I had only known I would have held her for as long as was needed. I would have held her forever.

CHAR TRITT'S STORY

Char Tritt has lived in Lake Oswego, Oregon, since 1977. She retired from her profession as an occupational therapist in 2013. She enjoys her four grandchildren, travel, art, bridge, quilting, and volunteering at church. Participating in memoir writing class has been a rewarding experience.

I'd Rather Be Flying

By Char Tritt

S OMETIMES IN SUNNY WEATHER WHEN THERE IS NO WIND, I GAZE
at the airplanes in the sky and remember how it felt to see
the earth from the air.

My first interest in flying came as a teen when I read a
series of books about a sixteen-year-old girl who earned her
pilot's license and her ensuing adventures. I also read about
Amelia Earhart and other female pilots. I did not give much
more thought to flying again until I was working as an occupational therapist in a school for handicapped children in
Orange County, California. One of the teachers had his pilot's
license and taught a ground-school class at a community college. I signed up for his class just to learn more about flying.

Partway through ground-school class, the instructor passed
out coupons to take one flying lesson for only five dollars. It
was at Orange County Airport, just minutes from work and
my apartment. I rarely pass up a chance to use a coupon and I
thought one lesson might help with my ground-school class, so
I took advantage of it. Normally, a plane rental and lesson in

1975 would cost about seventeen dollars an hour. I intended to just take one lesson to use my coupon.

During the first lesson, I learned how to taxi the plane to the runway and my instructor, a navy pilot recently out of the service, was already talking about how the second lesson would be to practice landings in the sky. So I decided to take two lessons. The instructor talked me through the elevations and rates of descent needed to simulate landing at 2,000 feet above sea level at a certain mark on the altimeter. We practiced landings in the sky that way for a few lessons. I remember him saying one sky landing was very good. "You only landed fifty feet below the runway that time, so you're ready for a real landing on your next lesson," he said.

So I decided to take a couple more lessons and landed the plane smoothly on about the sixth lesson. The lessons were in a two-seater Cessna 150, with two wheels in the back and one in the front and a high wing. At first, landings took intense concentration—lining up the plane in the center of the runway, landing on the back two wheels, then gently letting the nose wheel touch. Soon I developed a feel for it, similar to how a person learns dance steps of "left/right" and counting "1-2-3," until it becomes second nature, and the dance steps flow to the music. The landings were similar. The instructor had more confidence in my abilities than I did and was most encouraging.

About this time, in October of 1975, my boyfriend Tedd (now my husband) was transferred to a job in Portland, which left me with a lot of spare time in the evenings and weekends. I was flying up to four times each week. The instructor always spoke about the next lesson. I learned about making turns, doing "touch-and-gos," getting into a stall and recovering from a stall and landing on grass and other emergency maneuvers. After three months and twenty lessons, I was able to make my solo flight, a most exciting day, on January 3, 1976. Before I could tell my instructor that I was at a good stopping point, now that I had done my solo, he said I was nearly ready to do one cross-country flight. This is a short trip with the instructor to any airport within two hours. I chose to fly from Orange County airport to Chino airport where friends lived, so they could record my landing on their video camera. I do not recall why my start was delayed but when they greeted me in Chino, they said, "You are just like the airlines—two hours late!"

Next came the longer cross-country trip. That was about three hours long, all by myself to Santa Ynez/Porterville airport near Solvang, California, a village with Danish bakeries and souvenir shops. Friends met me at that airport and drove me to the Danish village for lunch, then I flew back to Orange County by myself. It was windy that day and I was advised to maintain 14,000-feet altitude to avoid the turbulence at lower altitudes. It crossed my mind that I was right at the borderline requirement for needing oxygen, which I did not have with me. So I was very relieved to land back at Orange County Airport.

By that time, co-workers were teasing me that I was addicted to flying. I told friends at work that "I can quit whenever I want, but I just don't want to quit flying." I remember saying, "I know that's what smokers say, but really I'm not addicted." I had confidence in my instructor so was not afraid to try new things. I was still looking forward to the next lesson without a firm decision to get my pilot's license. He had memorable words of wisdom like, "There are bold pilots and there are old pilots but there are no bold, old pilots." Or regarding the two rows of colored night landing guide lights: "Red over white, you're right, white over red, you're dead."

Then one day as I was visiting my dad and admiring a poem about flying, "High Flight," on a plaque on my dad's office wall, I asked him if I could have it if I got my pilot's license. He said, "Okay, but I know you will not get your pilot's license because I never got one." He encouraged us to be better than average but never better than he was, even when playing miniature golf. So I decided, "I'll show him," and became very motivated to get my license from that moment on.

In December, I needed to get some hours flying at night and enjoyed the colorful Christmas lights on the houses and boats below along the canals at Newport Beach and the marinas. Then at Christmas, Tedd and I became engaged. We planned to get married and move to Portland in April 1976. That gave me just under four months to get my license. I knew it would be best to finish with the same instructor and a familiar airport.

At that time, Orange County Airport was the second busiest airport after O'Hare in Chicago. It was good practice to take off and land there, giving the jets and airlines lots of space, and avoiding wake turbulence. Most lessons were in a Cessna 150, but a few lessons were in a Cessna 172 with four seats. One lesson was way beyond my requirements, but I was curious about it. I wondered, what did a spin or dive feel like? With my instructor expertly doing the dive maneuver, I was able to experience what three Gs felt like. I felt gravity pulling my checks downward and mouth open during the dive. It was interesting once, but I had no desire to become a stunt pilot or to try it again. Some days when it was cloudy or rainy and people would say that the sun was not out, my flying instructor would take the plane up through the clouds and there was the sun, shining brightly. It helps to remember that on gloomy days—the sun is shining if you can rise up above the clouds.

In April of 1976 I received my private pilot's license, got married, went on a two-day honeymoon and moved to Portland all in the same week! The plaque with the pilot's poem was given to me with a "good job" comment from Dad. It was displayed proudly on the living room wall of our new apartment in Portland. Once settled, I began working three days per week as an occupational therapist. It gave me some extra money and time to pursue flying. I needed to take more lessons to orient myself to the new setting of Portland and landmarks around the Troutdale Airport and the Evergreen Airport in

Vancouver. Before landing at Troutdale, pilots had to call the tower to say they were making a final turn and approach at "the farm," a green water tower. I asked the instructor why the term "farm," and he explained it had been a poor farm in the days before Social Security. Now it is part of McMenamins, Edgefield Hotel. There were many more new landmarks to get used to around Portland. I also practiced a soft landing on a grassy field at Mulino Airport.

Since I was new to Portland and needed some contacts and activities, I was happy to join a group of women pilots called the Ninety-Nines. The international organization of women pilots started in 1929 with ninety-nine women pilots and Amelia Earhart as its first president. It was educational as well as social, and had service projects to promote flying. In addition to monthly meetings, one of the service projects of the Columbia Cascade chapter of Ninety-Nines was to help the Red Cross by flying blood to outlying communities. Women with planes were encouraged to fly with a co-pilot, so I volunteered a couple times to be a co-pilot and meet a woman with her plane at McMinnville Airport. The Red Cross worker would come to the airport with a cooler, to be flown to Roseburg or another small airport where there was a need. The Red Cross would pay for the gas, and pilots would get some flying time, a "win-win" for all.

Another service project was to paint numbers on the runways of small airports. In 1980, about fifteen of us used stencils and roller brushes to apply white paint numbers at Aurora Airport. The numbers corresponded to the headings of the compass. Another service project, advertised to the public, was an evening program to help women overcome a fear of flying. The meeting was held in an airport hangar where someone gave a short talk about how much safer flying was compared to driving, followed with a chance for women to touch the plane, familiarize themselves with parts of the plane, and, if they felt comfortable, sit in the co-pilot's seat or the pilot's seat. If they wanted, they could even make an appointment to taxi in a plane at a later time.

Women shared some of the reasons for their fear of flying, most related to wondering how a heavy plane stays aloft. The one fear I remember most vividly was given by a young woman who had recently married a pilot. He owned a small plane, and, as he was flying with her on their honeymoon, he faked having a heart attack. When she screamed and panicked, he laughed. So she said she would never fly with him again! No one could blame her. One person suggested she might consider taking a few flying lessons so she could feel comfortable landing the plane if ever needed. I do not know if our class helped her or not. We certainly did sympathize with her.

The fundraising event of the year was a "fly-in" pancake breakfast at Dietz field in Canby every Labor Day weekend. Old bi-planes and small planes of all types would fly in. People would eat at tables set up outside along the small taxiway, and then fly out again. At least one hundred planes came. The houses along the Dietz runway looked normal from the street, but in addition to their garage, many would have a hangar for their plane out back. Several parties were held in homes there and everyone seemed to have a wooden propeller mounted over the fireplace.

Women of all ages were in the Ninety-Nines group. One sixty-year-old grandmother received an airplane as a birthday present from her husband, an onion farmer in Gaston. We played a variety of party games, such as making paper airplanes and giving a prize to the longest flight. Some of the pilots were married and brought husbands, often pilots themselves, to parties. It was a group of fun-loving people.

One highlight of those days was flying a seaplane. While on vacation at Lake Quinault, Washington, we saw a sign for "Sea Plane Rides." Since I kept my logbook and pilot's license in my car, the pilot said he would be happy to let me fly after he took off from the lake. It was a Cessna 172, so my husband sat in the back seat. In the air, it handled exactly like other 172 planes I had flown. The pilot let me fly while he explained how much harder take-offs and landings are because of needing to look for the current, logs, and other hazards in water. So I was happy enough that he put an entry in my logbook that I handled the seaplane while in the air, a credit for a lesson. He handled the landing.

As my work hours increased, my flying became like that of a "Sunday driver." I took friends and relatives for scenic flights over the house, or towards Mt. Hood and other close-in views of Portland. After having my pilot's license about four years, and having logged just over 100 hours, my priorities changed more toward career and starting a family, so I gave up flying in 1980.

Now it is too expensive to think of renting a plane, and my reflexes are not what they used to be, so I would not consider flying again. I would be happy to be a passenger in a small plane if the opportunity came up.

For many years, my car license plate holder stated, "I'd rather be flying." Even now on a sunny clear day, with no wind, I will look up at the small planes overhead and think, "It is a great day to fly."

LARRY A. TYLE'S STORY

Larry A. Tyle was born and raised in Portland, Oregon. He graduated from Grant High School and later from Oregon State College in 1983. Now retired from a career in medical malpractice insurance, he focuses on writing poetry and flash fiction. His work has been published in the *Statesman Journal, Northwest Passage, 5th & G Review*, and included in *Almost Twins*, a book of poems created by his recently deceased sister, Portland poet Judith Massee. He lives in Salem, Oregon.

Trial by Fire

By Larry A. Tyle

I WAS NINE, MY FRIEND, ALSO NAMED LARRY, WAS SEVEN. A vacant lot just around the corner served as a retreat center for our gang. Here we could escape the mandated behavioral expectations of our parents and comportment required by neighborhood mores. Our sanctuary was sited deep in the center of the lot obscured by shrubs and tall grass. By July, we had created a fort made out of boards and tarpaper scavenged from back yards. We were prepared to defend our fortification with real army equipment brought home and donated to the cause by World War II veterans who were family friends. At the time, it didn't seem to matter that the gear was German army issue, retrieved from European battlefields.

One sunny afternoon late in July, Larry and I set out for our duty at the fort. He had brought a box of wooden matches for no specific reason other than that they were conveniently left in his folks' kitchen. We discovered that, by cupping one match in the hand and flinging it head-first onto the sidewalk, you could create a fascinating miniature fireworks display not unlike setting off a ladyfinger. Ladyfingers were expensive and could deplete your allowance, if any, in a matter of minutes.

(There are times in one's life when you tempt fate and fate readily enters into the bargain, creating unexpected consequences, consequences laden with pain and subsequent disfavor and guilt; one might name these events intersections.)

At the intersection of 51st and Broadway, the locale of our fort, one small flaming match intersected with dry grass. And whoosh, conflagration! As we fled in terror, Engine #27 passed us, followed by Engine #19, the hook and ladder truck, the J. W. Stevens disaster car, and two police cruisers.

After the fire was extinguished, news of the event activated the neighborhood gossip mill, whereby the main culprit was identified as living at my address. Therein, the lord of the household, whose genetics held the wrath of Viking warlords, brought it upon my person, as to be felt even today.

Acknowledgements

I would like to thank the following for helping make this book possible:

The Lake Oswego Adult Community Center for offering memoir classes and for their support and flexibility in expanding the program to serve the needs of aspiring memoirists;

The *Lake Oswego Review* and the *Oregonian* for publishing some of our essays during the past few years;

Inkwater Press for providing in-person guidance and support during the final stages of this project;

And, of course, all the talented writers who filled these classes and shared their personal stories with strangers who became colleagues and friends.

In Memorium

I had the good fortune to meet Carmilla Fraser Marbaugh (January 10, 1915–March 12, 2018), in her 100th year. She was introduced to me by her wonderful granddaughter Anna, who has inherited her writing skills and taken them to new heights. Carm gave me a copy of her 500+ page memoir entitled *By All the Means You Can*, which she wrote at age ninety. She apologized for not having updated it. Her persistence and life-affirming attitude continue to inspire me.

CPSIA information can be obtained
at www.ICGtesting.com
Printed in the USA
FFHW02n1915250818
48004852-51706FF

9 781629 015729